Globalization and International Education

Also available in the Contemporary Issues in Education Studies Series

Also available from Bloomsbury

Globalization and International Education

Robin Shields

Contemporary Issues in Education Studies

BLOOMSBURY

LONDON • NEW DELHI • NEW YORK • SYDNEY

Bloomsbury Academic

An imprint of Bloomsbury Publishing Plc

50 Bedford Square	175 Fifth Avenue
London	New York
WC1B 3DP	NY 10010
UK	USA

www.bloomsbury.com

First published 2013

British Library Cataloguing-in-Publication Data
A catalogue record for this book is available from the British Library.

ISBN: HB: 9781441150196
PB: 9781441135766

Library of Congress Cataloging-in-Publication Data
A catalog record for this title is available from the Library of Congress.

Typeset by Newgen Imaging Systems Pvt Ltd, Chennai, India
Printed and bound in India

Contents

Series Editors' Preface

The series *Contemporary Issues in Education Studies* is timely for its critical exploration of education in this period of accelerating change. Responding to this challenge, the books in the series have titles that correspond closely to the needs of students taking a wide range of courses and modules within Education Studies and related fields such as teacher education. Education Studies is an important subject area that should be at the heart of many faculties of education. There is a need for relevant, core texts within Education Studies, which explore and critique contemporary issues across the discipline and challenge prevailing discourses of what education is about. We also need to provide students with strong theoretical perspectives and frameworks, focusing on relevant literature in an accessible and readable format.

We set the authors of this series a number of challenges in terms of what to include in their text. Therefore, each book addresses a contemporary issue in education and has an international rather than just an English focus. The texts are structured to provide a clear grasp of the topic and to provide an overview of research, current debates, and perspectives. Contextualized extracts from important primary texts ensure readers' exposure to dominant contemporary theories in the field of education, by demystifying essential vocabulary and educational discourse, enabling the education student to engage with these texts in a meaningful way. The extensive and appropriate literature review in each text gives a firm base for contextualizing the subject and promoting understanding at multiple levels.

This series is grounded in a strong conceptual, theoretical framework and is presented in an accessible way. Each book uses approaches such as case studies, reflective exercises, and activities that encourage and support student learning. Key relevant and contemporary questions are inserted throughout each chapter to extend the readers' thinking and understanding. Furthermore, additional material is also provided in the companion website to each book.

Robin Shields is Senior Lecturer in Education Studies (Global Education) in the School of Education at Bath Spa University, UK. He obtained his BA at the University of California, Santa Cruz, United States, and his Ph.D. also at the University of California, Los Angeles, United States. His teaching and research interests broadly focus on international development and the globalization of education. Robin has worked in international development, mainly in Nepal. Moreover, this has included research consultancy for UNESCO and working as programme coordinator for NGO Relief International. Furthermore, his work and research involves the use of Information and Communication Technologies (ICT) for education in low income countries. Robin's current research concerns international student flows in higher education, examining what the patterns in these flows reveal about larger processes of globalization.

Robin's book provides a contemporary focus on global and international educational issues. The importance of comparative education is underlined through similarities and differences that develop our understanding of our own educational professional practice. Robin's thematic approach also relates to more than two counties and that global reach is, we both feel, one of this book's advantages and strengths. The author also encourages the reader to use individual chapters as stand-alone texts rather than reading the whole book sequentially. We also feel that the book offers much more than an in-depth introduction to global and international issues in education studies. As we have asked all of our other authors, Robin also provides examples of critical analysis of assumptions, values and beliefs that underlie both education policy and practice. His book will appeal to both researchers and practitioners across a range of academic subjects and we feel that the market for this book will truly be international.

Since this is the last book in our series, we would like to thank all the authors of the seven books. We would also like to thank the teams at Continuum/Bloomsbury who have always been helpful and understanding as we have both worked within increasingly changing education environments. We continue to ask both our readers and students to keep thinking critically and have open minds to the possibilities and opportunities in relation to contemporary issues in education.

Simon-Pratt Adams
Richard Race
Chelmsford and Athens, July 2012

Acknowledgements

I have enjoyed a great deal of support from my colleagues at Bath Spa University in writing this book. I would like to thank Dan Davies, Stephen Ward, Alan Howe, Andy Bord, Graham Downes, Fiona Maine, Darren Garside, Christina Slade, Jodi Anderson and Christine Eden.

I am also extremely lucky to enjoy the support of inspiring and committed colleagues around the globe, who have been vital in helping to develop the content for this book. I would like to thank Jeremy Rappleye, Stephen Carney, Edith Omwami, Val Rust, Tejendra Pherali, Susan Robertson, Karen Edge, Terra Sprague, Richard Budd, Lizzi Milligan, Patrick Turner, Chiao-Ling Chien, Amy Armstrong, Rebecca Edwards and Mahabir Pun for their encouragement and support.

I would also like to thank Richard Race and Simon Pratt-Adams, the series editors, for their guidance, and David Blundell for his essential role in making this book possible. In addition, I am very thankful to Alison Baker and Rosie Pattinson at Bloomsbury for their support, patience and commitment and the team at Newgen for their dedication and attention to detail.

Finally, I would like to thank my family for their support during the writing of this book, particularly my wife Gayatri, and my daughter Nandini to whom this book is dedicated.

Abbreviations

ASEAN	Association of South East Asian Nations
AusAID	Australian Agency for International Development
CIDA	Canadian International Development Agency
DANIDA	Danish International Development Agency
DFID	Department for International Development (United Kingdom)
ECTS	European Credit Transfer System
EFA	Education for All
EHEA	European Higher Education Area
FFE	Food for Education (Bangladesh)
FTI	Fast-Track Initiative (World Bank)
GATS	General Agreement on Trade in Services
GDP	Gross Domestic Product
GTZ	*Gesellschaft für Internationale Zusammenarbeit* (German Agency for International Development)
HDI	Human Development Index
ICT	Information and Communication Technology
ICT4D	Information and Communication Technology for Development
IIT	Indian Institute of Technology
IMF	International Monetary Fund
INEE	Inter-Agency Network for Education in Emergencies
ITU	International Telecommunication Union
JICA	Japan International Cooperation Agency
KAM	Knowledge Assessment Methodology (World Bank)
KEI	Knowledge Economy Index (World Bank)
MDG	Millennium Development Goals
NGO	Non-governmental Organization
NORAD	Norwegian Agency for Development Cooperation
OBHE	Observatory on Borderless Higher Education
OECD	Organization of Economic Cooperation and Development
OLPC	One Laptop per Child
PISA	Programme for International Student Assessment
PRSP	Poverty Reduction Strategy Paper

STEM   Science, Technology, Engineering and Mathematics
TIMSS   Trends in International Mathematics and Science Studies
TRIPS   Trade-Related Aspects of Intellectual Property Rights
UNDP   United Nations Development Programme
UNESCO   United Nations Educational, Scientific and
           Cultural Organization
UNICEF   United Nations International Children's Emergency Fund
USAID   United States Agency for International Development
VLE   Virtual Learning Environment
WSIS   World Summit on Information Society
WTO   World Trade Organization

Introduction

Learning and knowing

In the traditions of Zen Buddhism, a *kōan* is a short story that promotes contemplation and guides meditation. Consider the following *kōan* recorded by Nyogen Senzaki in 1919:

> Nan-in, a Japanese master . . . received a university professor who came to inquire about Zen. Nan-in served tea. He poured his visitor's cup full, and then kept on pouring.
>
> The professor watched the overflow until he no longer could restrain himself. 'It is overfull. No more will go in!'
>
> 'Like this cup', Nan-in said, 'you are full of your own opinions and speculations. How can I show you Zen unless you first empty your cup?' (Senzaki, 1919/2010)

This *kōan* illustrates a key theme of this book: it shows that learning is often the process of 'unknowing' what one thinks one knows. Freire (1970) points out that although some conceptualizations of education focus on the acquisition of new facts and information, it is often the act of questioning previously held beliefs that is more important and worthwhile. To use the metaphor of the *kōan*, no learner has a completely empty cup; she or he will come to any educational setting with a set of values, assumptions and beliefs that are built upon a lifetime of experience as well as wider social and cultural traditions. Often these beliefs and assumptions are unrecognized by the learner; education is the process of critical analysis and reflection that reveals them.

Applied to the context of international education, the metaphor of the *kōan* has particular relevance. When studying the education system of another country or culture, a common set of questions often arises: Which country has the best education system? What set of educational policies and practices work best? However, these questions contain assumptions and implicit values that limit and constrain one's understanding. To ask which country has the best education system presupposes that 'good education' in one country is also good for others; to ask what works best assumes that policies and practices that work well in one country will also work well in others.

In the spirit of the Zen *kōan*, this book critically analyses the assumptions, beliefs and principles that underlie educational policy and practice on the global level. It discusses key issues and trends that are either international (involving two or more countries) or global (involving large parts of the world) in scope in a way that identifies what Nan-in calls 'opinions and speculations' (Senzaki, 1919/2010). Ultimately, the book contributes to an understanding of how education both constitutes and is shaped by the wider world.

Comparative and international education

The study of education in other societies is not new: examples of philosophers comparing education systems date back to writings from ancient Greece, and for many centuries the writings of travellers abroad included detailed descriptions of how foreign societies educated their youth (Phillips and Schwiesfurth, 2008). However, it was not until the publication of *Equisse et Vues Préliminaires d'un Ouvrage sur l'Éducation Comparée* (*Sketch and Preliminary Views for a Work of Comparative Education*) by Marc-Antoine

Jullien in 1817 that the term 'comparative education' first emerged, and not until the late nineteenth century that academics began to speak of comparative education as a distinct field of study (Bray, 2003). Since then, activity in the field has steadily increased: beginning with the Comparative and Education Society in the United States, societies and organizations devoted to the study of comparative education were founded in many countries. The year 1957 saw the publication of the first issue of *Comparative Education Review*, the first academic journal devoted to the study of comparative education and a leading journal in the field even today (Bray, 2003). By the 1960s, many universities had established professorships, courses of study and academic departments related to comparative and international education (Phillips and Schweisfurth, 2008). Today there are many journals devoted to comparative education (including *Comparative Education, Compare, Research in Comparative and International Education*, the *International Review of Education* and others), and academic societies and conferences devoted to comparative education enjoy strong memberships and attendance (Carney, 2010).

Early work in the field of comparative education was guided by practical concerns as scholars sought to find educational policies and practices that could be borrowed or assimilated in their own national context. Reflecting this priority, in 1900 Michael Sadler, an early researcher in comparative education, asked 'What can we learn from the study of foreign systems?' (cited in Steiner-Khamsi, 2004b:201). While such practical questions remain important, the field has also expanded to address issues of a more academic nature. Thus, contemporary research in comparative education examines the relationship between education and other aspects of society across different countries, and seeks to explain differences, commonalities and trends.

As an academic field of study, comparative education has been characterized by its interdisciplinary nature. Rather than relying exclusively on its own body of theory, comparative education draws upon and synthesizes theoretical perspectives from other disciplines, including sociology, history, economics, political science, history and anthropology. This interdisciplinary approach is both a weakness and strength: on the one hand research draws upon key topics and theories from these other disciplines, meaning that there is sometimes little overlap and engagement within published research, which has given rise to criticisms that the field is ill-defined and lacks focus (Philips and Schweisfurth, 2008; Novoa, 1998). On the other hand, the interdisciplinary approach has also ensured that researchers have constant access to new ideas, theories and methods from a number of academic fields, ensuring contemporary relevance and preventing isolation.

This interdisciplinary nature is complemented by a pluralistic approach to methodology and epistemology. Researchers have taken vastly different (often opposing) views on what constitutes valid knowledge and on how that knowledge should be obtained. Much research (e.g. Kandel, 1935; Holmes, 1981) has been guided by a humanist, interpretive approach to research, which uses qualitative data and historical analysis to situate a country's education system within its national sociocultural context (Arnove, 1999). However an alternative approach – first advocated by George Bereday (1957) – argues for a research paradigm that more closely resembles the methods of the physical sciences (Phillips and Schweisfurth, 2008). Rather than interpreting qualitative data, this approach involves analysis of variables (e.g. enrolment rates, economic output) across many countries (Arnove, 1999). The goal of this approach is to establish relationships between these variables that exist outside and independent of any national context, or as Harold Noah (2006) argues, 'to get rid of the names of countries . . . and substitute . . . the names of variables'. While differences in methodology persist in the field today, heated debate on the topic has gradually subsided, replaced with a pluralism that recognizes the respective strengths and limitations of each approach (Phillips and Schweisfurth, 2008).

The field of comparative education is founded on certain assumptions; to use the metaphor of the *kōan*, its cup not entirely empty. In particular, the very notion of comparative research is founded upon the belief that societies (including nation-states) are discrete, separate entities that can be isolated and compared with one another. However, contemporary social life is characterized by interactions that cross national boundaries: the *kōan* illustrates how key educational moments are often the result of an encounter between two different cultures (in the case of the *kōan*, the cultures of Zen Buddhism and Western academia). In response to this, Sklair argues that contemporary societies 'cannot be adequately studied at the level of nation-states, that is, in terms of each country and its inter-national relations, but instead need to be seen in terms of global processes' (Sklair, 1999:143). This conceptualization challenges the comparative perspective, which has traditionally used the nation-state as the unit of analysis, and requires an approach to studying education on the global level.

Global discourses on education

One way in which educational thought and practice have transcended the boundaries of the nation-state is through discourses on education that have become global in their reach. Consequentially, much of this book is devoted to the analysis of discourses on aspects of education, but the concept of 'discourse' itself is a complex one. It is rendered more opaque by its ambiguity: writers use the term 'discourse' in different ways and understand it to mean different things (Phillips and Jørgenson, 2002).

In the strictest sense, the term 'discourse' refers to the use of language in everyday situations, including both spoken and written language (Fairclough, 1995). It originates in the field of applied linguistics, which differentiates the study of language as it is actually used (in speech and writing) from the study of its underlying grammatical structure (Phillips and Jørgenson, 2002). However, discourse analysis goes beyond linguistics, as 'texts can never be understood or analysed in isolation – they can only be understood in relation to webs of other texts and in relation to the social context' (Phillips and Jørgenson, 2002:70). Thus, a key focus of discourse analysis is on understanding how language relates to the wider social context in which it is situated.

In this sense, discourse encapsulates not only patterns of language use, but also the worldview – the understandings, opinions, beliefs, and assumptions – that gave rise to them. Within this worldview, certain 'facts' are regarded as common sense, as axiomatic principles that do not need justification or explanation (Fairclough, 1995). To use the metaphor from the Zen *kōan* that opened this chapter, discourse is the tea that was in the professor's cup. To illustrate this concept, consider the following three examples of the discourse on 'world-class' education (italics added by author):

- 'If we hope to maintain a *world-class* economy . . . we will need *world-class* schools' (Gove, 2010): Michael Gove, secretary of state for Education in England and Wales, writing on the United Kingdom's performance on the OECD's Programme for International Student Assessment (PISA – see Chapter 6).
- 'Countries are striving to develop *"world-class* universities" that will spearhead the development of a knowledge-based economy' (Salmi, 2009:18): a report from the World Bank titled *The Challenge of Establishing World-Class Universities*.

- 'A *world-class* education is the single most important factor in determining not just whether our kids can compete for the best jobs but whether America can out-compete countries around the world' (Whitehouse, 2011): US President Barack Obama speaking at an education roundtable discussion on 18 July 2011.

All three examples invoke a common discourse of world-class education, but what is more significant than the phrase itself is the common set of understandings that they share. In all cases, education is linked to the creation of skills that enable a country to compete in the global economy. The discourse on world-class education embeds certain values: education is associated with economic benefits and purpose, free market economics and international competition are accepted as the natural order of the world. While these beliefs are not specifically articulated, it is precisely this tacit acceptance – a foundation of 'common-sense' that does not need to be defended – that characterizes the discourse.

In addition to revealing implicit worldviews, discourse analysis also provides insight into relationships of power. French social theorist Michel Foucault (1975) argues that powerful groups are able to control discourse, to normalize certain ideas and values while excluding alternative conceptualizations of reality. As a result, struggles for social power are fought in the domain of discourse, as competing interests vie to establish their respective worldviews as natural, logical and inevitable. For example, there are many alternative discourses to that of world-class education discussed above: one could argue that a world-class education promotes social cohesion, ethical behaviour, or environmental sustainability. However, powerful actors (in this case politicians and the World Bank) are able to dominate this discourse to promote one particular view of world-class education: that which produces global economic competitiveness. Alternative discourses are marginalized through their omission from prominent documents, policies and speeches.

The example of world-class education also demonstrates how certain educational discourses have become global in their scope; both patterns of speech and the worldviews that give rise to them are shared by individuals and institutions around the world. Although those quoted on world-class education share no formal relationship, they hold a common view of education that transcends and exists independently of national boundaries and national education systems. Analysis of these discourses provides one way to overcome the limitations of a state-centric comparative approach and understand education from a truly global perspective.

Overview of the book

This book provides a discussion and analysis of contemporary issues in education studies that are global or international in scope. It does so through a thematic approach: each chapter introduces a key topic, discusses important aspects of that topic, and illustrates its relevance through concrete examples. Strictly speaking, an international topic is one that relates to two or more countries, but most of those discussed in this book involve many countries throughout the world. Many are 'global' in the sense that they are not the result of the policies or efforts of any single country, government or organization. For this reason, the book is not comparative in its approach although it does draw extensively upon research from the field of comparative education.

The book is intended primarily for students of Education Studies, although it is also suitable for those studying related subjects (e.g. sociology, international relations, political science) – trainee teachers, educators and practitioners, and readers with a general interest in the subject matter. In order to support a variety of learning contexts, group discussion questions are included at the end of each chapter. While the chapters are intended to be read sequentially, readers seeking specific information on a particular topic could consult individual chapters without reading the entire book.

The first three chapters are devoted to one prominent discourse on international education: that of education and development. Combining historical and thematic approaches, Chapter 1 looks at how the link between education, economic growth and national development was constructed in the decades following World War II. Chapter 2 looks at shifts in the discourse on education and development in recent decades, with more emphasis placed on education as a human right and a means to poverty reduction. Chapter 3 discusses critical perspectives on education and international development, showing that the very concept of development is much more complex than is often acknowledged. Chapter 4 introduces an emerging area of research: the relationship between education and conflict. This topic is complemented with a discussion of a new field of practice: the provision of education in conflict-affected and post-conflict societies.

The final four chapters focus on the globalization of education: increasing convergence, integration and international flows in educational policy and practice throughout large areas of the world. Chapter 5 begins this discussion by looking at theoretical perspectives on globalization: while scholars generally agree that education is increasingly globalized, they provide differing and often opposing explanations of why this is occurring. Chapter 6 analyses the new importance placed on education in discourses on the global knowledge economy, with particular emphasis on international achievement tests. The following two chapters examine aspects of globalization and education in greater depth: Chapter 7 discusses information and communication technology (ICT) in international education, and Chapter 8 discusses the globalization of higher education.

These chapters offer the reader an in-depth introduction to global and international issues in Education Studies. Of equal importance, they provide a critical analysis of assumptions, values and beliefs that underlie educational policy and practice. This forms an excellent starting point for further independent research and analysis or professional work in related fields.

Useful websites

http://baice.ac.uk – The British Association for International and Comparative Education. Last accessed on 4 May 2012.

http://bit.ly/ComparativelySpeaking – A documentary on the first 50 years of the Comparative and International Education Society produced by Teachers College at Columbia University. Last accessed on 4 May 2012.

http://cies.us – The Comparative and International Education Society. Last accessed on 4 May 2012.

Education and International Development

1

Chapter Outline

Introduction

In the latter half of the twentieth century, a new way of conceptualizing education took hold. In many parts of the world – particularly in European colonies that had recently won independence – education was linked to countries' social and economic development. As part of this conceptualization, a new field of practice in international education emerged, which sought to spur improvement in living standards by increasing the availability and quality of education. This chapter discusses the emergence of international development education as a domain of theory and practice. It begins by describing education in colonial societies and then turns to early work in international development following World War II. The chapter gives an overview of key theories that informed early development work and describes the growth of development organizations at the national and international levels. Finally, it offers two illustrative case studies that demonstrate how the expansion of education was associated with development efforts in Nepal and Zambia.

Education and colonial rule

If one had used the term 'international development' at the turn of the twentieth century, it is doubtful whether it would have been clearly understood by anyone. Any form of systematic cooperation between countries to reduce poverty and create economic growth throughout the world did not yet exist. Instead, colonial models of governance dominated international politics: the great majority of Africa and Asia were ruled by European powers, either directly or indirectly. Britain ruled most of contemporary India, Pakistan and Bangladesh, as well as large parts of Africa and the Caribbean, while France controlled much of west and north Africa. By 1914, Europe's major colonial powers controlled 35 per cent of the world's land area (Bassett and Winter-Nelson, 2010:109).

In the eyes of European colonial powers such as Britain, France and Belgium, the colonial relationship was mutually beneficial and natural: colonized societies benefited from supposedly superior European governance, while the colonizing countries obtained access to low-cost raw materials and basic labour. 'Development', or the systematic improvement of living conditions in colonized societies, was a relatively minor aspect of this relationship. Although colonial government came to accept some responsibility for the welfare of colonized people, the extent of development was relatively limited and never intended to put colonized territories on equal footing with European countries (Abbott, 1971).

Education figured largely in the policies and activities of colonial governments. For example, the British colonial government in contemporary India established educational administrations that took some responsibility for starting schools, although priority was given to the children of British parents. By the turn of the twentieth century, universities had been established in Calcutta and Mumbai, although less than 5 per cent of the population received formal education (Gallego, 2010:228). Lord Curzon, viceroy and governor-general of India, speaking at a conference in 1905, laid out a vision for education in India that focused on employment and national progress, claiming:

> Education is required not primarily as the instrument of culture, of the source of learning, but as the key to employment, the condition of all national

advance and prosperity, and the sole stepping-stone for every class of the community to higher things. (Karkaria, 1907:47–8)

However, in other areas, education was linked directly to the oppression of colonized societies. Thus, Cecil Rhodes, a British politician and businessman who controlled large areas of southern Africa through his business interests, believed that:

> We have got to treat the Natives where they are, in a state of barbarism. We are to be lords over them . . . The Natives should be a source of assistance to the white man as labourers. This must be the main purpose of his education. (Cited in Bassey, 1999:32)

Colonial rule viewed anything more than the minimum level of education necessary to ensure operation of the colony as dangerous: educated members of society were likely to make demands for employment suiting their skills. Thus, Curzon claimed that 'the Indian University turns out only a discontented horde of office seekers, whom we educated for places which are not in existence for them to fill' (Gosh, 2007:383).

Across many colonial territories, particularly those in Africa, the work of European Christian missionaries included a number of educational activities. Missionary education centred on religious content, but the curriculum was sufficiently broad to include the provision of basic literacy and numeracy skills. The impact of missionary education was profound: according to one estimate, 99 per cent of all African schools in 1942 were established by missionaries (Coleman, 1958), and many of these are still in operation today.

Birth of the 'development era'

The close of World War II marked a turning point in international political relationships: due to the heavy toll of war and growing political awareness in the colonies, European powers could no longer maintain their empires. Beginning with India in 1947, one colony after another gained political independence from colonizing European powers, often only after considerable struggle. However, the rapid withdrawal of European governance created its own set of problems: former colonies were left with new, often unstable governments, limited infrastructure, and economies that were highly dependent on trade with colonial powers (Presbich, 1959; Escobar, 1995).

In his 1949 inaugural address, US President Harry Truman proposed a new agenda for relations with former colonies that would greatly raise their standards of living by extending industry and free market capitalism. The speech came at a crucial time in world politics; while colonial empires (especially those of Great Britain and France) were beginning to decline, two new competing superpowers, the capitalist United States and the communist Union of Soviet Socialist Republics (USSR), were on the rise. In his speech, Truman called for a foreign policy that would:

> Make available to peace-loving peoples the benefits of our store of technical knowledge in order to help them realize their aspirations for a better life. And, in cooperation with other nations, we should foster capital investment in areas needing development. Our aim should be to help the free peoples of the world, through their own efforts, to produce more food, more clothing, more materials for housing, and more mechanical power to lighten their burdens. With the cooperation of business, private capital, agriculture, and labour in this country, this program can greatly increase the industrial activity in other nations and can raise substantially their standards of living.
> (Inaugural Addresses, 2009:113)

 Truman's speech reflected the values and worldview that would guide work in international development over the next half century. It defined democracy, scientific knowledge and economic growth as the keys to all countries' prosperity and progress. Furthermore, Truman's speech represented a new view on living conditions in former colonies. In contrast to Rhodes's earlier view of poverty in southern Africa as a consequence of what he termed 'barbarism', Truman believed that 'humanity possesses the knowledge and skill to relieve the suffering of these people' (Inaugural Addresses, 2009:112). Instead of a natural condition, poverty became a technical problem that could be addressed through science, democracy and industrialization.

The founding of the United Nations in 1945, to promote good will between countries and coordinate a range of international affairs, marked another important milestone in the emergence of international development. Echoing Truman's sentiments, its founding charter contained a mandate to promote 'conditions of economic and social progress and development' as well as 'solutions of international economic, social, health, and related problems' (United Nations, 1948). This laid out a clear vision for development that linked economic factors to health and social problems, and it created the first coordinated international effort to address these perceived problems.

The newly founded United Nations was supported by a range of financial institutions, most notably the International Monetary Fund (IMF) and the World Bank (formally called the International Bank for Reconstruction and Development). These were originally founded to stabilize international trade and to finance the reconstruction of countries decimated in World War II, but in later years they would go on to play an important role in international development (Kapur et al., 1997).

Even with fresh memories of the horrors of World War II, an uneasy new stand-off between two major global powers came to be known as the Cold War. At the heart of the Cold War were ideological differences in political economy: one side, led by the United States, believed in free market capitalism and multiparty democracy. The other side, led by Soviet Russia, advocated centrally planned economies and the global solidarity of communist parties. Cold War politics quickly transformed international relationships, as Western Capitalist and Soviet powers sought to extend their influence to other parts of the world (Escobar, 1995). The term 'Third World' emerged to describe countries – many of which were former colonies – that were not aligned to either free market capitalism (i.e. the 'first world') or Soviet communism (i.e. the 'second world' – D'Aeth, 1975). For several decades, United States' foreign policy stressed that the spread of communist models of government in Third World countries should be actively opposed, using force if necessary.

The effect of Cold War politics on international development was twofold: on the one hand, the ideological battles of the Cold War prompted the outbreak of real wars in the Third World (e.g. Korea, Vietnam and Afghanistan), in which rival factions (e.g. North and South Vietnam, North and South Korea, Afghan factions) were backed by capitalist and Soviet powers. On the other hand, both sides in the Cold War started large-scale aid programs as part of their foreign policy. Aid became a key tool in promoting good will, gaining political influence in strategically important areas, and promoting the two respective models of political economy in the nonaligned Third World.

Thus, by 1950 'international development' – the systematic intervention in and restructuring of other countries in order to improve their standard of living – had emerged as a new area of foreign policy and international relations. In the coming decades, it was supported by a growth in academic fields of study (e.g. development economics) and governmental agencies (e.g. the World Bank and USAID).

Human capital and modernization theories

While Truman's foreign policy and the UN Charter created lofty goals for the international community, it was unclear how these goals would be accomplished. The new concept of international development created a mandate for changes in a number of areas, including health, governance, finance, industry, agriculture and education. Among these, the last had a special significance, as investments in education could yield benefits in the remaining areas. For example, an educated population could provide skilled labour to support the growth of new industries.

The use of education to create economic growth was supported by a new body of economic theory defining the concept of human capital. As defined by economist Jacob Mincer in 1958, human capital refers to an individual's traits and abilities that are economically productive (Mincer, 1958). For instance, knowing how to build a house, run a business or programme a computer are all forms of human capital. Mincer's work compared the lifetime income of males in the United States with differing levels of education, and found that those with more education earned considerably more, even when the expense of additional education was taken into account. Education was then a way of creating human capital: investment in education would eventually yield economic return in much the same way that deposits in a savings account would yield interest. More simply put, human capital theory substantiates the proverb, 'give a person a fish, feed them for a day; teach a person to fish, feed them for a lifetime'.

While Mincer's work related to education in the United States, human capital had a strong influence on those in the newly forming field of international development. American economist W. W. Rostow believed that investment in human capital would put countries in the Third World on a path to economic take-off and prosperity. Rostow (1960) put forward a set of ideas about how countries develop, which collectively came to be known as modernization theory. Rostow's modernization theory states that countries pass through the following five stages as part of their development:

1. Traditional society
2. Preconditions to take-off
3. Take-off
4. Drive to maturity
5. The age of high mass consumption

According to Rostow (1960), 'traditional societies' are characterized by agricultural economies, hierarchical social arrangements and a lack of science and technology. However, by meeting certain preconditions, including education and a strong national government, these 'traditional societies' are able to undergo a 'take-off' and eventually become industrialized, affluent countries. While education was not the only precondition to take-off, it was one of the key factors that would allow a country to create a high-growth, industrial economy.

Modernization theory had a significant effect on early work in international development. Rostow himself held positions in the cabinets of US presidents John F. Kennedy and Lyndon Johnson, and his ideas were highly influential in the newly formed United States Agency for International Development (USAID – Pearce, 2001). However, the 'take-off' that Rostow predicted failed to materialize in many countries – evidenced by persistent poverty even in countries that received large amounts of development aid (Escobar, 1995). It also bears the mark of Cold War politics, as Rostow continually points out the benefits of American model of free market capitalism over Soviet communism (Pearce, 2001).

Both human capital and modernization theories have left a lasting legacy on the development sector. Their impact is less visible in terms of concrete institutions and policies than in the way that development is conceptualized and discussed in society at large. For instance, development organizations (e.g. the UN, USAID and DFID) often speak about development in terms of growth and economic opportunity, and investment in education is seen as a necessary precursor to development (World Education Forum, 2000). These ideas are often taken to be so fundamentally true, that they do not need explanation. Thus, a the claim of UNICEF executive director Anthony Lake that 'ending the cycle of poverty for children, their families and their communities begins with education' is immediately understood to link education, growth and development, even without explicitly saying so (United Nations, 2010).

Reflective Exercise

- In your own words, define development. What does it mean for a society to be developed? Is education necessary for development, and is it sufficient to ensure development?

Aid agencies

The emergence of the field of international development brought with it the birth of a new form of governmental bureaucracy. In the decades following World War II, both the newly formed United Nations and the governments of affluent countries created departments whose main mission was to provide development funding and technical assistance. As an emergent world leader and contender in the Cold War, the United States was first among these, creating USAID in 1961. The United Kingdom followed suit, creating the Ministry of Overseas Development in 1964. After a series of reclassifications under successive Labour and Conservative governments, it was renamed the Department for International Development (DFID) in 1997. In the following decades, similar governmental agencies were created in many industrialized countries, including Denmark (DANIDA), Australia, (AusAID), Japan (JICA), Norway (Norad), Germany (GTZ) and Canada (CIDA).

The United Nations declared the years 1960–70 as the 'Development Decade', in which its members would 'intensify their efforts to mobilize and sustain support for... developing countries to progress towards self-sustaining growth of the economy' (United Nations, 1961:17). Part of this effort involved consolidating its existing programmes for international assistance into the United Nations Development Programme (UNDP) in 1965. While UNDP's perspective emphasized economic growth, investing in people, through education and healthcare, was also a focus of its early work (Murphy, 2006). UNDP was supported by two other agencies: the United Nations Educational, Scientific and Cultural Organization (UNESCO), and the United Nations International Children's Emergency Fund (UNICEF). While these organizations were created for specialized purposes, they would both become more involved in the international development efforts in the coming decades.

However, the role of the UN was somewhat overshadowed by the a rapid growth and transformation of the International Bank for Reconstruction and Development, more commonly known as the World Bank, which was founded alongside the UN in 1945 to finance the reconstruction of European countries decimated in World War II. In 1960, the Bank introduced the International Development Association, a specialized department dedicated to international development (Jones, 2006). Since then, the Bank has gone on to become the largest provider of development finance in the world. However, unlike many other development agencies, the World Bank operates not as a donor, but rather as a lender: its funding is generally in the form of loans that needed to be repaid, sometimes with interest. This means that most work funded by the World Bank needs to be financially viable, and countries that borrow money are ultimately responsible for paying it back (Jones, 2004).

The Bank initially concentrated its investments in infrastructure financing (e.g. constructing bridges and dams). The established view was that lending for education and health programmes was too risky, as returns were largely unknown, with one Bank president exclaiming, 'we can't go messing around with education . . . we're a bank' (Kapur et al., 1997:111). However, evidence of high rates of return from lending in social services prompted the World Bank to make its first loans for education programmes in 1963. Its early education programmes focussed on technical and vocational education, as these were assumed to yield the highest and most direct economic returns (Kapur et al., 1997:796). Throughout the 1970s, lending for education increased more than threefold, from $62 million per year in 1968 to $590 million in 1980, constituting 14 per cent of all World Bank funding (Kapur et al., 1997:258, 346).

Reflecting the basic tenets of human capital theory (Mincer, 1958), the Bank believed that investments in education would create a productive workforce that would be able to repay the initial loan and interest. As Jones (2004:189) states, World Bank lending policies 'provide a window on what global capital has to say about economic and social policy. In particular, it illuminates those ideas that global capital is prepared to back with finance'. By investing in education with an expectation of financial returns, World Bank funding tested human capital theory on a scale and at a cost that had never been attempted before. However, the results were not as straightforward as might have been hoped, and in the countries where investment in education did not yield the desired result, governments were left with large debts and growing interest (Jones, 2004).

The proliferation and growth of national aid agencies, UN organizations, and the World Bank created a two-fold structure for international development funding that persists today. One side of this structure consists of bilateral aid, or development assistance that is given directly from one country to another. This is usually done through national aid agencies (e.g. DFID or USAID) and may relate to the larger diplomatic and historic ties between the two countries. For instance, many countries in which UK's DFID operates are former colonies of the British Empire (DFID, 2012). Bilateral aid can be linked to recipients' support for the donor's position on pressing international and global issues (Fleck and Kilby, 2006), demonstrating the politicized and controversial role of aid. The other side of development financing consists of multilateral aid, development assistance that comes from an international organization (e.g. UNDP or the World Bank). In some sense, bilateral and multilateral aids are really two sides of the same coin: since international organizations are funded by their member countries, any development aid they provide comes indirectly from these governments.

Case studies: Nepal and Zambia

The birth of international development created a global revolution in educational practice. Many newly independent colonies established national education systems as a first order of business, and as a result the number of students enrolled in schools increased throughout the world. In 1950, there were approximately 253 million primary school students in the world, approximately 47 per cent of all children. By 2006, this figure had more than doubled to 654 million, or 86 per cent of all eligible children. However, growth was even more dramatic in former colonies; for instance, primary school enrolment in sub-Saharan Africa increased from 20 per cent to 70 per cent between 1940 and 2006 (Benavot and Riddle, 1998:200–3; UNESCO, 2008:307). This boom in enrolment rates is often referred to as the expansion of mass education (Boli et al., 1985), as in many countries access to education expanded from a privileged few to 'the masses' (i.e. most of the population).

In many senses, Zambia exemplifies the experiences of many former colonies in sub-Saharan Africa. Under British rule, some education was provided by missionaries and the colonial government. As the economy was heavily focused on copper mining, there was little need for skilled labour, and as a result only 961 Zambians in the entire country had completed secondary school at the time of independence (Kelly, 1991:13). After independence, the government prioritized secondary and technical education in the hope of increasing economic growth, with secondary enrolment tripling between 1964 and 1969. This meant that primary education received less attention than might have been hoped for, despite a government goal to ensure at least four years of schooling for every child (Kelly, 1991:14).

While the country experienced a decade of strong economic growth, fluctuations in the global price of copper weakened the government and prompted it to request assistance from the IMF and World Bank (Kelly, 1991:20). At the time, both institutions required borrowing countries to undergo a series of reforms collectively known as structural adjustment. These conditions included minimizing spending on public services (including education), and promoting free trade with other countries. Zambia entered into a structural adjustment agreement with the World Bank and IMF in 1983, which stipulated limits on public sector pay, removal of agricultural subsidies, and allowing free exchange of its currency internationally. Effects of structural adjustment policies caused considerable turmoil within the country, including wide fluctuations in the price of food that sparked riots (Simutanyi, 1996). Combined with a growing HIV/AIDS epidemic, limits on public expenditure contributed to a drop in school enrolment from 80 per cent in 1980 to 68 per cent in 2000 (World Bank, 2012a).

In contrast to Zambia, the Himalayan kingdom of Nepal was never directly ruled as a colony. Instead, its rulers held it in near isolation from the outside world for nearly a century, partly to avoid the influence of the British rule in India. However, when its neighbour India became independent in 1947, Nepal opened its doors to the outside world, establishing diplomatic relations with other countries for the first time (Whelpton, 2005). Due to its strategic location (between communist China and democratic India), it was able to leverage a sizable amount of foreign aid from competing world powers, and, as a result, it received proportionally more aid than other countries in the region. Like Zambia, it became heavily dependent on foreign aid, and by the 1980s these funds accounted for 40 per cent of the overall government budget (Whelpton, 2005:128).

Like Zambia, Nepal quickly took steps to establish a national education system. Within 50 years, literacy expanded from 2 per cent to 49 per cent and primary school enrolment jumped from a mere 9,000 to over 3.6 million (UNDP, 2004; World Bank, 2001). For the national government, education was a key in developing a cohesive nation: as Nepal contained many different ethnic, linguistic and religious groups, maintaining national unity was perceived to be a major challenge. Thus, a commission convened by the government to lay the foundations for a national education system proclaimed 'schools and educational systems exist solely for the purpose of helping the youth of a nation to become better integrated into the society' (Nepal Education Planning Commission, 1956:14). While the effort to build a single nation was largely successful, by doing so the government marginalized many linguistic and religious minorities. Through its policies and curriculum, the government successfully promoted the idea that these minority groups were backward or deficient, while Hindus who spoke the national Nepali language were forward-looking and progressive. Simmering tensions about the rights of minority groups were among the causes of a decade-long civil war that broke out in 1996 (Shields and Rappleye, 2008a: see Chapter 4).

What is perhaps most remarkable about the global expansion of mass primary education is not how individual countries differed in their approaches, but how similar they were. Throughout the world, schooling was implemented using more or less the same model: schools were built, teachers were trained, and students entered classrooms that would have looked quite familiar to a European visitor. Furthermore, most governments placed priority on primary education, preferring to provide basic education to as many people as possible rather than offer secondary or higher education to a few. In both cases, international organizations (e.g. the UN and World Bank) were deeply involved in the development of education systems throughout the world. Their roles went well beyond simply providing funds for education; they also gave recipient countries advice on how their education systems, and indeed their entire economies, should operate.

Reflective Exercise

- Did education lead to development in Nepal and Zambia? What does their experience say about the relationship between education and development?

Summary

The latter half of the twentieth century witnessed the rise of the international development sector, bringing with it new government agencies and international organizations (see Appendix – International Education and Development Timeline). Education played a pivotal role in the new development sector: Rostow's (1960) modernization theory stipulated that investments in education would put Third World countries on the path to development, eventually transforming them into industrialized societies similar to those in Western Europe and North America.

However, the experiences of Zambia and Nepal show that the relationship between education and development is not straightforward or deterministic. Zambia initially concentrated on secondary and technical education, but was later hard-hit by structural adjustment programmes and burdened with debt. Nepal's history shows not only that primary education can be rapidly expanded in just a few generations, but also that this expansion can marginalize many groups within a society.

The most important outcome of the post-war period was a set of ideas about what development is and what it means to be developed. These were articulated by development theorists such as Rostow (1960) as well as through international development organizations (e.g. UNDP, World Bank, USAID). The notions that former colonies should develop into industrial nations, that international aid could facilitate the economic growth required, and that investments in education were one way they could do so, all emerged during this period. More than 60 years later, these ideas still underlie much of the work within the field of international development as well as the ways in which development is constructed in popular media and the press. However, the next chapter examines how challenges to these underlying ideas have redefined development work and the role of education within it.

Reflective Exercise

- What does it mean for a country or society to be 'developed'? Form groups and come up with a list of characteristics or qualities that you think a country should have to be considered 'developed'. Then take a critical look at each characteristic and try to find exceptions: are there countries that are considered developed that don't meet these criteria? Conversely, are there countries often considered 'developing' or 'Third World' that do meet the criteria?

Useful websites

http://50.usaid.gov – A history of USAID's first 50 years. Last accessed on 4 May 2012.

http://blogs.worldbank.org/education – World Bank blogs on education. Last accessed on 4 May 2012.

http://eldis.org – A database of international development research. Last accessed on 4 May 2012.

http://worldbank.org – The World Bank's website. Last accessed on 4 May 2012.

www.dfid.gov.uk – The United Kingdom's Department for International Development. Last accessed on 4 May 2012.

2 Redefining Development: Education for All

Introduction

Since the beginning of state-provided education in Europe and North America, the prospect of education for all children in the world has formed a key part of visions of a fair and equitable society (Benavot and Riddle, 1988). This chapter looks at how the Education for All (EFA) movement has become a key component of international aid and development. It begins by discussing a paradigm shift in the international development sector; after several decades of work guided by modernization theory (Rostow, 1960), priorities shifted away from economic growth towards poverty reduction as the ultimate goal of development work. The chapter then traces the history of the global EFA movement through from the 1990s to the 2010s and discusses three key issues: gender, funding and language. It analyses the implementation of EFA in Bangladesh as a case study and concludes with a summary of the chapter.

Redefining development: from growth to poverty reduction

The previous chapter showed that in a span of several decades, the field of international development grew rapidly; institutions (e.g. the UN and World Bank) were formed, supported by a body of academic theory (Rostow, 1960), and funding for education and other development programmes began. However, in their hurry to begin tackling the problems of underdevelopment, donors (e.g. World Bank and USAID) largely assumed that economic growth through industrialization and capitalist economic models were the best means to improve standards of living (Escobar, 1995). For this reason, they concentrated almost exclusively on economic growth as a measure of countries' development (Sen, 1983).

However, the work of Sen (1983, 1999) shows that the notion of development is much more elusive and complex than the relatively linear conceptualizations of modernization theory acknowledged. Sen (1999) looks at the correspondence between income and measurements of quality of life (e.g. life expectancy, access to education) throughout the world and finds that the two often vary in unexpected ways. For instance, he points out that the per capita gross domestic product (GDP – a measure of economic productivity) of Brazil ($2050) was nearly ten times that of Sri Lanka ($270), yet on average Sri Lankans lived three years longer (Sen, 1999). Furthermore, specific groups in affluent societies were more deprived than citizens of developing countries; for example, Sen (1999) also uses the example of African Americans in the United States, who have considerably lower life expectancies than those of people in China or the Indian state of Kerala.

Based on this evidence, Sen (1999) argues that the concept of development needs to be redefined; rather than measuring development in terms of economic growth, he proposes that it should be measured by the freedoms, opportunities and rights of individuals, which he collectively terms capabilities. Sen's concept of capabilities includes entitlements such as access to healthcare and education, as well as liberties such as the right to vote and freedom from persecution.

Sen's capabilities theory of development (for which he earned a Nobel Prize in economics) had important implications for the international development sector (Sen, 1999). First, it decreased the emphasis on economic growth as a measure of development; Sen provides evidence that high economic output is not necessary to create a high quality of life. To be sure, a certain level of income is required to ensure adequate shelter, nutrition and health, but beyond this basic level of subsistence the benefits of income become increasingly minimal. This view marked a clear departure from the established field of development economics, which focused on creating high rates of GDP growth in developing countries. It also emphasized other rights and other social dimensions to development; Sen showed how the right to vote, to speak one's language, and to obtain employment without discrimination were all important components of development. These were often considered internal political matters and had previously received little attention in development work. Thus, the capabilities theory moved the focus of development away from economic growth and towards equity, social inclusion and poverty reduction.

This shift in development priorities slowly permeated development institutions, shifting their priorities towards poverty reduction. Among the first was the UNDP; in 1990 it developed the Human Development Index (HDI) as a way of measuring and comparing development in different countries. The HDI differs from other development measures (e.g. GDP per capita) in that it takes a holistic view of development; it is computed using a complex combination of income, education and life expectancy statistics. The UNDP uses the HDI in its annual *Human Development Report* (e.g. UNDP, 2010), a widely read publication that broadly surveys measures of development (e.g. life expectancy, enrolment and GDP) throughout the world.

The World Bank followed suit in changing its focus to poverty reduction. Throughout the 1980s, it had developed stringent structural adjustment programmes that required borrowing countries to privatize public services and open their doors to international trade. Influenced by the economically conservative policies of Thatcher and Reagan, these had been widely criticized as having a destabilizing effect on developing countries; public services were underfunded while cheap foreign imports undercut the prices of local farmers, leading to wide fluctuations in prices of commodities.

Partly recognizing their failure, the Bank ended structural adjustment programmes and instead adopted the practice of Poverty Reduction Strategy Papers (PRSPs – World Bank, 2011). PRSPs are essentially a blueprint to reduce poverty within a borrowing country, specifying programmes that are needed and how they will be funded. In the Bank's own words 'PSRPs describe a country's macroeconomic, structural and social policies and programs to promote growth and reduce poverty, as well as associated external financing needs' (World Bank, 2011). As the name suggests, the primary goal of PRSPs is poverty reduction, although this is often linked to economic growth. Furthermore, the process of creating PSRPs claims to be more participatory, as 'they are prepared by governments through a participatory process involving civil society and development partners, including the World Bank' (World Bank, 2011).

Thus, by the 1990s a clear shift had taken place in development theory and practice: economic growth was no longer an end in itself, but rather one of several means of poverty reduction. The latter entailed elements that were non-economic in nature: human rights, equity and social inclusion. Nevertheless, much work in the development sector continued to emphasize economic growth, although now this was under the rationale that high rates of growth would reduce poverty. However, in the field of education the shift to rights-based development marked a clear change in the role and purpose of education in development.

The right to education: education for all

Corresponding to the redefinition of development in terms of equity, inclusion and poverty reduction, there was a shift in the rationale for supporting education. Early work in international education by organizations such as USAID and the World Bank was rooted in human capital theory (Mincer, 1958), which justified spending on education on the grounds that it would later yield economic return. However, the increasing emphasis on equity and inclusion by UNDP and the World Bank required that all individuals have access to education, even if no immediate economic benefit could be foreseen. Thus, the discourse on education and development began to emphasize education as a fundamental human right rather than an economic investment.

The notion that education was a right of all individuals was not entirely new; many countries in Europe and North America had begun to provide universal education to their citizens over the previous two centuries (Benavot and Riddle, 1988). However, until the mid-twentieth century, extending this right to education to a global scale had received little attention. The 1948 UN Declaration of Human Rights changed this, guaranteeing the right to basic education (using the term 'elementary education') by proclaiming:

> Everyone has the right to education. Education shall be free, at least in the elementary and fundamental stages. Elementary education shall be compulsory. (United Nations, 1948)

The Declaration was an important step in establishing education as a right; it was ratified by a near unanimous vote of the General Assembly and therefore provided a unifying basis for addressing human rights on an international level. However, in practice it did little to support or enforce this declaration; a comprehensive, coordinated effort to provide education for all would not come for several decades.

The first decade of EFA: Jomtien to Dakar

The shift towards a rights-based perspective on education and development culminated in the World Conference on Education for All, which was held in Jomtien, Thailand in March 1990. Organized by UNESCO, UNDP, UNICEF and the World Bank, the conference was attended by representatives from 155 countries and 150 organizations. Delegates to the conference drafted and adopted the World Declaration on Education for All, a landmark documented that committed participating countries to providing universal access to primary education (i.e. education for all) by the year 2000.

The shift towards a rights-based perspective on development is clearly evident in the Jomtien Declaration; it begins by 'recalling education is a fundamental right for all people, men and women, throughout the world' (World Conference on Education for All, 1990:2). It also emphasizes social equity and inclusion, with special attention to the rights of indigenous groups, linguistic minorities and disabled people. Gender received particular attention; the declaration stipulated 'the most urgent priority is to ensure access to, and improve the quality of, education for girls' (World Conference on Education for All, 1990:5). The emphasis on equity and particular focus on girls' education have remained core aspects of the EFA agenda.

In order to coordinate and measure progress towards universal primary education, the delegates also authored a Framework for Action to Meet Basic Learning Needs. This called for regional conferences to measure progress and an EFA Assessment in the year 2000 to track global progress. However, it left many of the details of EFA implementation to national governments, claiming that 'progress in meeting the basic learning needs of all will depend ultimately on the actions taken within individual countries' (World Conference on Education for All, 1990:6).

At the time of the Jomtien Declaration, it was estimated that some 100 million children did not have access to primary school, 60 million of whom were girls (World Conference on Education for All, 1990:6). Over the following decade, primary school enrolment increased by 82 million, including 44 million girls, yet the 2000 EFA Assessment placed the number of out-of-school children at 113 million, representing an overall *increase* (World Education Forum, 2000:13). How did this happen? While governments expanded the overall number of places available, global population growth (particularly in developing countries), meant that the number of children without access to primary schooling was higher than in 1990.

EFA in the twenty-first century

While the Jomtien Declaration was not successful in universalizing primary education by 2000, it established education for all as a key item on the international development agenda. Following the 2000 EFA Assessment, the World Education Forum convened a follow-up conference in Dakar, Senegal in April 2000. The conference produced the Dakar Framework for Action, a document that renewed the pledge of universal primary education and extended the target date for EFA to the year 2015. It also set the following six goals that defined set the EFA agenda over the following 15 years:

1. Expanding and improving comprehensive early childhood care and education.
2. Ensuring that good quality primary education is free, compulsory and universally accessible.
3. Providing access to learning and life skills programmes for all young people and adults.
4. Achieving a 50 per cent improvement in levels of adult literacy by 2015, and access to basic and continuing education for all adults.

5. Eliminating gender disparities in primary and secondary education by 2005.
6. Improving the quality of education through measurable learning outcomes.
(World Education Forum, 2000:8)

The goals of the Dakar Framework and the renewed pledge for EFA received considerable boost from the adoption of the Millennium Development Declaration in September 2000. The Declaration set out eight Millennium Development Goals (MDGs) that essentially defined the global development agenda for the next 15 years; ranging from reducing HIV/AIDS to protecting biodiversity, the MDGs were agreed to by all 192 member countries of the United Nations. In order to ensure that progress can be measured and monitored, each goal was accompanied by a set of specific targets and accompanying indicators (e.g. enrolment ratios, literacy rates, girls' share of enrolment) that were used to measure progress.

Two of the MDGs were particularly relevant to EFA: the second goal, to 'achieve universal primary education' essentially reiterates the goals of Jomtien and Dakar, with a target that 'children everywhere . . . will be able to complete a full course of primary schooling' (United Nations, 2000). The third goal, to 'promote gender equality and empower women' is also relevant to EFA's goals, as the corresponding target is to 'eliminate gender disparity in primary and secondary education, preferably by 2005, and in all levels of education, no later than 2015' (United Nations, 2000).

Thus, the year 2000 marked both a failure to reach the goals of Jomtien and amplified calls to achieve the goal of EFA. This was not only in declarations from international conferences, but also in the support and resources available, particularly through international organizations. UNESCO has created several organizational mechanisms that meet annually to oversee and coordinate the EFA movement. These include an EFA Working Group of key members of the EFA movement and a smaller EFA High-Level Group, comprising representatives from national governments and development agencies. Both have met annually since 2000, and the Working Group sets the agenda for the High Level Group meeting. Additionally, since 2002 UNESCO has published the EFA *Global Monitoring Report*, a comprehensive document that tracks progress towards achieving the goals set in Dakar. Each year's report focuses on a different aspect of or challenge to EFA, including gender (UNESCO, 2003), literacy (UNESCO, 2006), governance (UNESCO, 2009) and conflict (UNESCO, 2011).

Key issues in education for all

While EFA has received a significant amount of attention and support in recent years, the goal of attaining universal primary education by 2015 remains a challenge. In fact, the 2011 *Global Monitoring Report* points out that 67 million children do not attend primary school and estimates that if current trends ~~progress~~ continue this will increase to 72 million out-of-school children by the 2015 deadline (UNESCO, 2011:6). A key priority for the EFA movement, therefore, is to identify obstacles to expanding enrolment and develop ways to overcome them. This section examines two key obstacles to achieving the EFA goals: gender and funding. It also looks at how the debate around minority language education involves a trade-off between expanding enrolment and protecting marginalized groups.

Gender

From the earliest days of the EFA movement, ensuring gender equality in education has been a key priority, driven by consistent data showing that most out-of-school children are girls (World Conference on Education for All, 1990). Between the Jomtien Declaration in 1990, and the 2000 EFA Assessment, the percentage of girls in out-of-school children remained relatively constant at 60 per cent, meaning there were three out-of-school girls for every two boys (World Conference on Education for All, 1990; World Education Forum, 2000). Since then, there has been some progress, with girls' share of out-of-school children dropping to 54 per cent. However, the 2005 deadline for achieving gender parity (i.e. equality in enrolment, or a 50% share of out-of-school children) specified in the Dakar Framework and MDGs has come and gone, and at the current rate of progress reaching the goal by 2015 appears dubious.

While data showing girls' underenrolment is clear, the underlying reasons are complex and multifarious. The 2003 *Global Monitoring Report* identifies decisions within the household as a key to explaining girls' underenrolment, as prevailing tendencies favour boys when only a limited number of children in the family can attend school. This is supported by data showing that in countries where enrolment is already low, the gender gap in enrolment tends to be higher (UNESCO, 2003), suggesting that when resources for education are scarce, girls will suffer more. However, the Report also points out that there are notable exceptions to this rule, including Zambia, Tanzania and Niger, meaning that it is not an inevitable outcome but rather the result of conscious decisions that can be countered through proactive policies and programming (UNESCO, 2003).

Labour is another way in which household decisions perpetuate the gender gap in education: research has shown that in many countries girls' share of household work is proportionally higher than boys. This includes unpaid work such as caring for younger siblings and small-scale agriculture as well as supporting the family economically through paid work outside the home (Herz and Sperling, 2004). The result is that girls are less available to attend school and more likely to leave primary school before completion. This is reflected in a larger drop between girls' primary and secondary enrolment in some countries. For example, in Togo, girls' primary enrolment is 80 per cent; while this is less than that of boys (90%), it is approaching gender parity (i.e. equal number of boys and girls in school). However, in secondary schooling school girls' enrolment drops to just 24 per cent, and there are nearly two boys for every girl in school, meaning that gender gap reappears when girls are unable to progress to secondary education, and girls' primary completion rates are also lower than boys' (UNESCO Institute for Statistics, 2011a).

A key question for those in the EFA movement is how to address the gender gap; if its causes are in pervasive social practices that exist across many cultures, it would seem that addressing the problem at the root is incredibly difficult. Some social norms and cultural values may work against girls education, for example the 2003 *Global Monitoring Report* describes how 'some Ethiopian fathers . . . noted that more educated girls face problems because they cannot find a husband or employment opportunities; they will get older, have to stay with their parents and bring shame upon the family' (UNESCO 2003:123).

Herz and Sperling (2004) put forward several strategies to close the gender gap in primary education. First, they argue that schooling must be affordable for girls, including not only the direct costs of schooling (i.e. school fees, books and uniforms) but also the indirect costs, including compensating families for girls' lost household work. They point to programmes in Bangladesh, Mexico and Brazil that provided stipend for girls from low-income families, and saw large increases in enrolment and participation. Second, they point out that schools need to be 'girl friendly', which includes having private toilet facilities for girls (many schools in low-income countries lack these), curricula that portray educated females in a positive light, and trained female teachers to provide a role model for girls in school.

As mentioned above, the most encouraging information on the gender gap is that statistics show that it is not inevitable. There are enough countries that have managed to reach parity in gender to show that it can be accomplished, even in countries that have struggled to provide universal education. However, achieving gender parity on a global scale remains an elusive target.

Funding

The Dakar Framework for Action made the pledge that 'no countries seriously committed to Education for All will be thwarted in their achievement of this goal by a lack of resources' (World Education Forum, 2000:9). However, funding education remains a major challenge in many low-income countries. Governments typically spend 1–2 per cent of their total national GDP on primary education (or 15–30% of the total government budget). However, in low-income countries spending the same proportion of the GDP on education will yield a much smaller total amount than in countries with more wealth. As a result, in many low-income countries' spending per student is less than $50 per year, while in the United Kingdom the figure is close to £3975 (UNESCO Institute for Statistics, 2005; Department for Education (UK), 2010).

In recognition of the difficulties faced in funding EFA, the World Bank established the Fast Track Initiative (FTI) in 2002. The FTI brings together international development donors in a special funding arrangement for EFA: countries that meet a series of requirements and develop a clear plan to achieve EFA are guaranteed to receive donor funding to finance their plan. Thus, the FTI offers a reliable source of funding for countries that meet eligibility criteria. However, this poses a problem for the larger EFA movement, as the most marginalized countries (i.e. those with very high rates of poverty and limited government capacity) are unlikely to be able to meet these eligibility criteria (Archer, 2004). Rose (2005) shows that many countries that were not eligible for FTI were at risk of not achieving EFA, while those that were eligible would likely have reached EFA goals anyway. As a result, she concludes 'the FTI has resulted in a selective approach of accelerating progress towards the goals in particular countries, including ones which appear to be already on-track to achieve them' (Rose, 2005:393).

Language of instruction

The pledges signed in both Jomtien and Dakar contain commitments to meet the needs of linguistic minorities, which clearly entail some provision of education in minority languages. Furthermore, research has shown that students who learn to read in their mother tongue first are able to learn to read in a second language more quickly than if they are first taught the second language (Mehrotra, 1998). However, to translate educational materials and train teachers who speak these languages takes resources and funds that might otherwise be used to expand access to out-of-school children (by building more schools and training teachers). Therefore, the language of instruction has become a thorny issue that pits equity against access.

The language of instruction is particularly relevant in sub-Saharan Africa, where many countries (e.g. South Africa, Zambia and Uganda) are highly multilingual with numerous indigenous African languages. Because of this multilingual composition, former colonial languages (e.g. French, Portuguese, Afrikaans) are used at the national levels, and English as a *de facto* international language. Brigit Brock-Utne (2001) points out that economic circumstances tend to promote the use of colonial languages at the expense of indigenous languages, as textbook publishers (who operate as for-profit companies) are most likely to concentrate their work in dominant languages (i.e. colonial languages or English) that will yield more sales than publications in indigenous languages. Brock-Utne (2001) further shows that while UNESCO supports the right to mother tongue education, lending policies of the World Bank have implicitly favoured dominant languages by reducing state funding for education and promoting the role of the private sector, meaning that the profit motive will inevitably gravitate towards dominant languages.

Reflective Exercise

- It appears that the 2015 goals of education for all will not be met. Where does responsibility for this lie – on international organizations, on donor countries or on national governments?

Case study: Education for All in Bangladesh

The experience of Bangladesh exemplifies both the struggles and successes of the EFA movement. Located in South Asia, Bangladesh is one of the most densely populated countries in the world and, as a low-lying tropical region, is susceptible to flooding and certain infectious diseases such as malaria (Rahman et al., 2007). UNDP's 2010 *Human Development Report* ranks Bangladesh 129th in terms of human development, placing it in the 'low human development' category but above most of sub-Saharan Africa. Particularly in rural areas, poverty levels are high and persist from one generation to the next; in the words of a recent study 'pervasive poverty has kept generations of families from sending their children to school, and without education, their children's future will be a distressing echo of their own' (Ahmed and Arends-Kuennig, 2006:665). However, the country also shows signs of becoming an influential economic power; high population growth has slowed in recent years while the economy has been strong since 2000. Reconciling new economic opportunities with high levels of poverty, particularly in rural areas, has been a major challenge facing the country.

Since the Jomtien conference in 1990, the government of Bangladesh has taken strong proactive measures to attain universal enrolment in primary school. A 1990 government act made primary education compulsory, and education-led poverty reduction was a key focus of the country's Fifth Five Year Plan (1997). Reflecting these priorities, expenditure on education increased from 5 per cent to 12 per cent of the government budget between 1990 and 2000 (UNESCO, 2000). The government also became less dependent on aid to finance education; in the same time period foreign funding of the education budget decreased from 19 per cent to 12 per cent (Kimura, 2003).

Education funding has been supported by special measures to target children in poverty. Started in 1993, the Food for Education (FFE) programme provided a grain ration to low-income families who sent their children to school. To receive the full ration, families had to send all children in the household to school, and children needed to maintain an attendance rate of 85 per cent. In 2002, the government replaced FFE with the Primary Education Stipend (PES) programme, which provides a cash stipend for low-income families who send children to school (Ahmed and Arends-Kuennig, 2006).

Bangladesh's progress towards universal primary education has been considerable: net enrolment has gone from 64 per cent in 1990, when the EFA movement began, to 91 per cent, in 2008 (World Bank, 2012a). However, achieving EFA by 2015 will be a challenge, although favourable economic conditions and slowing population growth create some space for optimism. One area in which Bangladesh has been particularly successful is gender equality; the country was able to achieve gender parity in both primary and secondary education by 2005. Data from 2008 show that 94 per cent of girls now attend primary school, while in 1990 the figure was just 59 per cent (World Bank, 2012b). This achievement is largely a result of proactive government policies: the terms of both FFE and PES helped to increase girls' primary enrolment (Ahmed and Arends-Kuennig, 2006), while other policies have eliminated fees and provided stipend for girls in secondary school.

As a case study, Bangladesh shows that considerable progress can be made towards the EFA goals, even in a relatively low-income country. Perhaps more importantly, its experience with EFA shows that gender equity can be achieved even before universal enrolment is achieved. It also shows that this was made possible by proactive government policies that actively countered the disincentives for girls' education discussed above. As a lesson for the EFA movement, Bangladesh shows that concrete government support is essential if EFA goals are to be achieved.

Summary

Beginning in the mid-1980s, a shift began to take place in international development; influenced by the work of Sen (1983, 1999), development organizations began to focus less on economic growth and more on poverty reduction, equity and inclusion. In the field of education, this is reflected in the EFA movement, an initiative to provide primary education to all children in the world by 2015. EFA is led by UNESCO, but is supported by a number of international organizations (e.g. the World Bank), national aid agencies (e.g. DFID) and non-governmental organizations (NGOs). The goals of EFA were first stated in the World Declaration on Education for All in Jomtien, Thailand in 1990, and then renewed in the Dakar Framework for Action in the year 2000 with a 2015 deadline.

Despite a large increase in primary students worldwide, progress towards EFA remains difficult. In 2008 there were 67 million children out of school and if current trends continue this will increase to 72 million by the 2015 deadline (UNESCO, 2011:6). Three key issues are especially relevant to the challenge of achieving universal enrolment. First, gender parity has been a priority for the EFA movement, as girls make up the majority of out-of-school children globally. Research (UNESCO, 2003) shows this is due to prevailing preferences to educate boys, particularly when resources for education are scarce and a larger share of household work is borne by girls. Funding is another key challenge, as in many countries funding for education is scarce. The debate around language of instruction is also important, as supporting minority languages benefits learners but demands extra resources (Brock-Utne, 2001).

Many of these issues can be seen in the case of Bangladesh, which has made great strides towards achieving the EFA goals. Although attaining universal primary enrolment remains a challenge, the country has achieved gender parity in primary and secondary education and increased overall enrolment. Increased funding for education, a strong commitment to poverty reduction, and policies that actively counter disincentives to girls' education have all contributed to this progress towards EFA goals.

Reflective Exercise

- Consider the following official policy statements on access to education, spanning over 350 years and much of the globe:

'It is therefore ordered, yet every township in this jurisdiction . . . shall then forthwith appoint one within their town to teach all such children as shall resort to him to write and read, whose wages shall be paid either by ye parents or masters of such children', Massachusetts Law of 1647 in the English Massachusetts Bay Colony.

'There shall be provided . . . a sufficient amount of accommodation in public elementary schools, available for all the children whose elementary education . . . efficient and suitable provision is not otherwise made', the 1870 Education Act in England and Wales.

'The State shall provide free and compulsory education to all children of the age of six to fourteen years in such manner as the State may, by law, determine', India's Constitution, written in 1949.

'By 2015, children everywhere, boys and girls alike, will be able to complete a full course of primary schooling', the UN's Millennium Development Goal #2, ratified in 2000.

Discuss why the education of all children has proven to be such an enduring goal for societies around the world. Do you believe that one day all children will attend school? How would this affect social and economic development?

Useful websites

http://data.worldbank.org – The World Bank's online database, with information on enrolment and literacy. Last accessed on 4 May 2012.

http://unesco.org.uk/education_for_all – Information on Education for All from the UK National Commission for UNESCO. Last accessed on 4 May 2012.

http://un.org/millenniumgoals – Information on the Millennium Development Goals. Last accessed on 4 May 2012.

Critiquing Education and International Development

3

Chapter Outline

Introduction

To many readers, the notion of development criticism may seem puzzling: if development aid provides money to the world's poorest people, why would anyone be against it? The very term 'development' inherently implies progress and improvement; to critique something that is by its definition a positive phenomenon seems illogical. However, work in the international development sector is deeply contentious, and the researchers discussed below have put forward compelling critiques of international development and the role that education plays within.

This chapter discusses and evaluates critiques of education and international development. It begins by conceptualizing critiques, distinguishing between those that seek to reform development efforts and those that reject the idea of development entirely. The chapter then proceeds to discuss critical perspectives on international development and education, beginning with the problematic relationship between donors and aid recipients, then continuing to Marxist, poststructuralist and postcolonial perspectives on development. The application of these critical perspectives is then demonstrated through the analysis of a television advertisement for a non-governmental organization.

Conceptualizing development critiques

Criticism of international development first emerged in the late 1950s (Presbich, 1959), and since then an animated dialogue of critical perspectives on development has continued to grow. The critics discussed in this chapter (e.g. Escobar, 1995; Klees, 2001; Said, 1978) have come from a wide range of academic and professional fields (economics, anthropology, sociology, etc.) and from both high- and low-income countries, and thus critical work on development represents a range of different viewpoints. Ironically, these critics disagree with one another in their fundamental beliefs and attitudes: for example, some (e.g. Sachs, 2005; Collier, 2007) argue that the major shortcoming of development has been insufficient aid from donor countries, while others (e.g. Escobar, 1995; Ferguson, 1990; Mohanty, 1991) argue that this aid itself is a major source of problems.

As a starting point, some critical perspectives accept the underlying tenets of development: that the lives of those in poverty can be improved through foreign aid and systematic social programmes that intend to create economic growth and improve standards of living (Sachs, 2005; Collier, 2007; Riddell, 2007). In this light, it is reforms to the implementation and practice of development that are needed to achieve international development goals. For example Sachs (2005) argues that current levels of development funding are insufficient, pointing out that if development donors were to meet their target of allocating 0.7 per cent of GDP to development aid, the extra funding generated would be sufficient to lift all people in the world out of dire poverty. Others such as Collier (2007) and Riddell (2007) argue that donors need to further reform their economic policy and approach to international relations for aid to be effective.

However, stronger versions of the reformist perspective point out that it is not only implementation that must be reformed, but also the reasoning, goals and values that underpin this work. For example, in the Indian state of Punjab, social activist Vandana Shiva (1989) has studied how development – particularly the growth of large-scale industrial agriculture – has led to widespread environmental damage and undermined the traditional place of women in society by replacing their central role in family-based, small-scale agriculture with industrial models of production. To Shiva (1989), this is not development at all, but actually quite the opposite. From this perspective, development is shown to have hidden or implicit biases in addition to commonly stated goals (i.e. poverty reduction, social inclusion and human rights) that compromise its overall legitimacy. Thus, 'true' development would require a fundamental shift not only in development practice and implementation, but also in the way that development itself is conceived.

Taking this even further, stronger critical perspectives reject the overall legitimacy of international development as a whole by exposing inconsistencies or contradictions in its fundamental assumptions and values. For example, Escobar (1995:6) argues that development is a 'regime of representation' that systematically portrays the developing world as backward and deficient. To Escobar and others (Ferguson, 1990; Mohanty, 1991), development is a guise, a thin veil used to mask relationships of power and hegemony. Ultimately, Escobar claims (1995:162), 'Development is about growth, about capital, about technology, about becoming modern. Nothing else'.

The critical perspectives discussed above entail very different implications for education: on the one hand, reformist arguments that accept the basic premises of development but seek to improve or reform its practice advocate expanding formal schooling in order to ensure that all children benefit from access to education. On the other hand, stronger critiques regard current models of formal schooling as a means of reproducing and expanding an inherently unjust system; instead of expanding education there is a need to 'deschool society' (Illich, 1971) – replacing curriculum-based learning with critical inquiry that identifies and combats practices of oppression (Freire, 1970).

Power, politics and the donor agenda

Development aid involves not only the transfer of funds, but also the transfer of ideas and policies from donors to recipient countries. A major critique of international development programmes is that they reflect the interests and priorities of donor organizations rather than those of aid recipients (Samoff, 1999; Brock-Utne, 2000). Chapter 1 examined how Structural Adjustment Programmes run by the World Bank and IMF required countries to reduce government spending and privatize public services in order to receive continued financial support. As many countries (e.g. Zambia – Fraser, 2009; Burkina Faso – Samoff, 2004; and Tanzania – Therkilsden, 2000) became entirely reliant on funding from these organizations, they had little choice but to accept these conditions, often with devastating consequences.

In the education sector, Jones (2004) has shown how the World Bank has yielded considerable influence in formulating the educational policies of loan recipients. Jones describes how the World Bank has viewed itself not just as development donor, but also as a 'knowledge bank', a provider of expertise about 'best practices' in education (Jones, 2004:189). Because World Bank funding is usually provided as loans that must be repaid (Jones, 2006), there is an imperative that the programmes it funds are those that will create the economic growth necessary to repay the loan. However, as views on education and development have changed over the years (see Chapter 2), the World Bank has been in the advantageous position of having full control over educational policy decisions while bearing little responsibility for their consequences. As Jones acknowledges, 'Many countries . . . have had to struggle for years to pay off Bank loans for purposes since discredited by the bank' (Jones, 2004:191). Regardless of whether one agrees with the overall goals of international development work, the political influence of development donors is ground for critique.

Even without direct political influence, development donors are able to exert their influence on national education systems in other, less direct ways. For example, in his study of non-governmental organizations (NGOs) and educational policy in Nepal, Rappleye (2011a:44) describes how 'donors use NGOs as instruments to influence macro-policies, education sector priorities and even ways of thinking about economics, development and society'. This case presents an ironic juxtaposition: donors have increasingly preferred to work with NGOs due to their participatory, grass-roots nature and because they provide a way to avoid direct engagement with recipients' state bureaucracies (Klees, 2001), yet, as a result, NGOs have become heavily reliant on competitively awarded donor funding, transforming them into agents of donors' interests. Thus, the relationship between aid and influence appears unavoidable, as wealth and power are inextricably linked.

Marxist perspectives and world systems analysis

As mentioned in Chapter 2, the past century has witnessed a rapid of expansion of enrolment in primary schooling throughout the world, particularly in low-income countries and former colonies (Benavot and Riddle, 1988). This is usually portrayed as uncontroversial, beneficial and a sign of social progress (World Conference on Education for All, 1990). However, as formal schooling has spread to every corner of the world it has carried with it a set of associated values. Building upon the notion of the 'hidden curriculum' (Jackson, 1968) – a set of values, behaviour and knowledge that is transmitted informally alongside the mainstream curriculum – Bowles and Gintis (1976) argue that formal schooling serves capitalist interests by preparing students for a lifetime of exploitative wage labour. In schools, children are taught to obey authority, to follow timetables, to maintain order and to produce work according to deadlines: all necessities for the workforce of a capitalist society.

If one accepts that formal schooling is associated with the reproduction of capitalist societies, then the spread of formal schooling throughout the world also expands capitalist models of social organization. Wallerstein's (1974) concept of world systems analysis charts this expansion: describing a single, integrated world capitalist system that has developed over the past four centuries. This began with trade in simple commodities (food and spices) and – as European countries accumulated increasing levels of capital – transformed first into the colonial world order and then the current system of transnational corporations, international finance and global integration.

In this world economic system, capital owners (whom Wallerstein terms the 'core') seek to perpetuate their advantage by increasing their capital through return on investments. As capital seeks growth, the world economic system must continually find means to expand, and one way to achieve this growth is by incorporating societies that have traditionally existed outside its reach. These societies, which are often based on sustenance agriculture and non-monetary exchanges of goods, are not initially amendable to capitalist investment and profit (Wallerstein, 1974), and thus a social and cultural transformation is required to integrate them into the world economic system. The mainstream portrayal of this transformation as development is ideological, reformulating the exploitative core/periphery relationship as one of cooperation: world systems analysis argues that international development is primarily an expansion of the world economic system (Arnove, 1980).

The documentary *Schooling the World: The Whiteman's Last Burden* (2011) addresses this very issue, making that provocative claim that 'if you wanted to change an ancient culture in a single generation . . . you would change the way it educates its children'. According to director Carol Black, the expansion of formal education has created a global 'monoculture' that embraces consumerism, non-sustainable use of resources, exploitation and excessive individualism. The film examines schooling in Ladakh, a remote area in India's Himalayan Mountains, showing how the expansion of formal education has systematically eroded and destroyed traditional cultural values and ways of life. The expansion of state education has resulted in students moving away from their family homes to urban centres; as instruction is in English, they rarely speak the indigenous Ladakhi language (which is banned in schools under the threat of punishment) and understand little of their cultural heritage. Despite these losses, children do poorly in national examinations and struggle to find jobs. The film ironically contrasts these experiences with speakers from the World Bank who extol the power of education as a means of development, poverty reduction and economic growth.

Reflective Exercise

- How can the right to basic education through formal schooling be in conflict with the right to maintain one's cultural and linguistic traditions? How should this tension be addressed in development work?

Poststructuralism, postcolonialism and the discourse of deficiency

Unlike Marxist perspectives, poststructural theory does not locate the basis of power in material wealth (i.e. capital), but rather posits that power exists in the ability to create and control knowledge. This refers not only to the academic knowledge produced by researchers and taught in educational institutions, but also to common-sense understandings, assumptions and taken-for-granted facts, which poststructuralists collectively refer to as a discourse (Jørgensen and Phillips, 2002; Fairclough, 1995).

Literary critic and social theorist Edward Said applies the poststructuralist perspective to an international context by arguing that the academic study of the cultures and languages of 'the Orient' (i.e. Asia, the Middle East and North Africa) by Europeans actively supported and contributed to the colonization of these areas (Said, 1978). In particular, Said shows how studying the Orient divided the world into two groups, an 'us' (Westerners) and a 'they' ('Orientals'), a category that essentially combines all non-Western cultures, despite their great differences. In his words,

> There are Westerners and Orientals. The former dominate, the latter must be dominated, which usually means having their land occupied, their internal affairs rigidly controlled, their blood and treasure put at the proposal of one or another Western power. (Said, 1978:36)

Said's work forms the foundation of a critical perspective known as postcolonialism, which seeks to explain current contemporary social practices as a reflection of continued political domination associated with Western colonialism (Bryan, 2008).

The postcolonial perspective holds immediate relevancy to development critique: just as colonial powers justified their rule on knowing what was best for colonized people, so too is development justified on a superiority of knowledge. Donors claim to know what development is, why it is desirable, and how it can be achieved. This claim to truth is supported by a body of academic research in disciplines such as comparative education, economics and international development studies, as well as the professional knowledge and practice of development workers. In contrast, those being developed lack the power and agency to construct, establish and perpetuate their own body of knowledge (which, if permitted, would likely highlight the inequalities, power disparities and cultural impositions associated with development; Escobar, 1995).

A key argument in postcolonial studies of education and development is that the legacy of European colonialism has resulted in a 'colonization of the mind' (Chiriyankandath, 2011:37). This colonization includes a persistence of 'Western' values in education (e.g. individualism as opposed to collectivism) as well as orientations toward history (which locate the origins of the contemporary world order in Western Europe) and constructions of knowledge (around Western science) that all reflect colonial powers rather than indigenous cultures (Shahjahan, 2011). Furthermore, the influence of donor organizations – particularly those that 'lay the "blame" for school failure at the local level' (Tikly, 2001:168) – continues the pattern of domination that existed under colonial rule (Lingard and Jn Pierre, 2006).

Case study: 'saving' Asha

To illustrate and exemplify the relationship between power and representation in development critique, this section analyses a television commercial for a major international non-governmental organization. The advert starts by showing a poverty-stricken girl, emaciated, gaunt, with a distant glazed look on her face. The narrator, an English male, reads

> Asha would ask you something if she could. She'd ask you to save her life, but she's too exhausted. She's starving. She'd look you in the eye; she'd ask again if she thought someone, somewhere had the heart to help.

Over footage of other starving children, accompanied by a slow, melancholy piano, the narrator continues:

> Please, help a child like Asha right now. We know what it takes to save a child's life. The solutions are simple, but we need your help . . . Asha can't ask you, but we can. Please will you stop children dying?

While Asha's story provokes feelings of pity, compassion and perhaps anger, disgust or guilt, these immediate reactions obscure deeper critical inquiry. The advert describes Asha's plight in great detail, but it leaves many other questions unanswered. First, where does Asha live? To many viewers, Asha's surroundings and skin colour suggest somewhere in Africa, but by leaving this unstated the advert places her in a vague, stereotypical Third World context. Second, why is she starving? Is it due to political oppression, or perhaps fluctuations in food prices caused by global markets? By not addressing this, the advert suggests this condition is an intrinsic or inevitable feature of living conditions in the 'Third World'. Even Asha's name raises certain questions: would the advert have the same impact if she were called Susan or Jennifer?

What is clear is that Asha's life is deficient, even pitiable in nearly every respect, but everything else is vague and unstated. Furthermore, the audience is continually reminded that Asha cannot speak for herself; instead, we must rely on the narrator to describe her plight. Thus, in this relationship the narrator (and by extension the development organization), hold all the power: they are able to put forward a representation that is remarkably one-sided: poverty is focused upon to the exclusion of all else.

Through this advert, one clearly sees the issues raised by poststructuralists such as Escobar (1995). Representation is asymmetric: the object of development (Asha) is represented by the narrator, who grounds his authority in

Poststructuralist

knowledge ('We know what it takes to save a child's life'). As Trudell (2009) notes, the primary feature of the development discourse is deficiency, often to the exclusion of all else. Thus, Asha is described only in terms of her problems and deficits. According to poststructuralists, the claim to save children like Asha is ultimately bankrupt; instead the concept of development is used as a guide to perpetuate a relationship of power and control.

Reflective Exercise

- How are issues of poverty and development portrayed in the media? How does this reflect upon the international development sector as a whole?

Analysis: three key questions

The critiques discussed above (i.e. donor interest, world systems analysis, and poststructuralism/postcolonialism) all differ in their fundamental theoretical and epistemological underpinnings. Furthermore, there is considerable overlap between critical perspectives, and heterogeneity within them. While this would appear to make comparing and evaluating development critiques very difficult, from a practical perspective the stance that one takes on development depends largely on a set of relatively simple questions:

1. Are there a set of universal values that should guide development efforts?
2. Are the values that underpin development efforts adopted by consensus or are they imposed by force?
3. Are global inequalities the result of exploitation or egalitarianism?

The first of these questions asks whether any set of values is universal; that is, whether there are moral and ethical imperatives that apply to all of humanity, regardless of differences in culture, religion or individual circumstances. If one answers in the affirmative, then this provides the basis for development initiatives (in education and other areas) that are global in their reach. The prevailing attitude in the international development sector is that establishing these universal values is simple and straightforward. Initiatives such as the Universal Declaration of Human Rights (United Nations, 1948), the Jomtien World Declaration on Education for all (World Conference on Education for All, 1990) and the Millennium Development Goals (United Nations, 2000) are all predicated on notions of the universal right to education. The moral basis and rationale for this universal claim is never problematized; the goals are clear. Rather, the focus is on the challenge of attaining them. In practice, however, these claims to universality prove deeply problematic. As shown in the documentary *Schooling the World* (2011), the right to education is often in opposition to the right to maintain one's cultural, religious and linguistic traditions.

The second question, then, is whether the underlying values of development are voluntarily adopted by aid recipients, or whether they are imposed by donors exerting power and influence. Here, it is important to consider not only those values often cited by development organizations (e.g. poverty reduction and economic growth) but also the possibility of 'hidden' values such as the expansion of capitalist models of social organization. Even if one accepts that the values of development have a universal basis, this does not mean that imposing them by force is justified, as this very act of imposition would violate these values. Nevertheless, the critiques of donor influence discussed above indicate that there is very clear evidence that this does occur.

The third and final key question refers to the vast inequalities that exist both within and between countries. If one accepts that the advantages enjoyed in high-income countries (longer life expectancies, better access to education, etc.) have been won through a fair and egalitarian process, then international development work presents a real opportunity to spread these fruits of success throughout the world. However, if the benefits of the privileged are at the expense of others, then constructing a relationship of aid and cooperation makes little sense. The high-income 'developed' world needs the 'underdeveloped' world in order to continue its affluent lifestyle. In this light, the notion of development assistance is tokenistic and ideological, used to mask and disguise a relationship of exploitation, yet Marxist, poststructuralist and postcolonial critiques of development all present compelling evidence that this is the case.

Summary

This chapter has presented and analysed critical research on international development and the role of education within it. The chapter began by conceptualizing critical positions, showing that some critiques accept the overall goals and values of international development, while others seek to reform them or reject the legitimacy of development altogether. The chapter examined three lines of critique in depth. The first (e.g. Jones, 2004) claims that development donors exert unfair influence over the policies of recipient countries because they control the flow of funding. The second critical perspective uses Wallerstein's (1974) concept of world systems analysis, which views development as an expansion of the capitalist world system, while the third (e.g. Escobar, 1995) utilizes poststructural and postcolonial theory.

Critical approaches were then illustrated through the analysis of text from a television advert produced by a major international aid organization. To make development critiques more approachable, three overarching questions were presented to the reader as way of theoretically orienting oneself to development critique. Seeking to explain some failings of education for international development, the next chapter focuses on a new approach to understanding international education: the globalization perspective.

Reflective Exercise

Consider the following three hypothetical scenarios, all of which relate to the right to education:

1. A girl in a rural village in Pakistan has dropped out of secondary school. Staff from an international development organization visit her house to encourage the parents to allow her to attend again. However, her parents say that it is against their cultural traditions for girls to go out the house unaccompanied at that age, and that her help is needed at home, they also point out that the girl herself does not want to attend.
2. A family has stopped sending their son to primary school. They are part of an ethnic/linguistic minority in their country, and point out that secondary schooling is only available in the national language. They are worried that if their sons keep attending school, their mother tongue will die out. They also don't feel a secondary education is relevant to their agricultural lifestyle.
3. A family in a poor, rural area take their second oldest boy out of primary school. They point out that times are very difficult, and unless this boy works in the fields, they will not be able to feed their other four children. Teachers point out that he will have no future if he leaves school, and that education is compulsory according to the law.

In each case, do you think the child in question should be required to attend school? Reflect upon whether age, gender or other circumstances (e.g. culture, family needs) influence your answer.

Useful websites

http://schoolingtheworld.org/film/trailer – The trailer and website for the film *Schooling the World*. Last accessed on 4 May 2012.

http://vandanashiva.org – Vandana Shiva's website. Last accessed on 4 May 2012.

4 Education in Conflicts and Emergencies

Introduction

The Education for All (EFA) movement is underpinned by the notion that education is generally beneficial for both individuals and society. Thus, the World Declaration on Education for All proclaims that 'education is a fundamental right for all people, women and men, of all ages throughout the world' and also that that it contributes to 'social, economic and cultural progress, tolerance, and international cooperation' (World Conference on Education for All, 1990). However, critical research has emphasized that education is more contentious than this optimistic view acknowledges, as it reproduces social inequalities, prejudices and forms of discrimination (Freire, 1970; Bowles and Gintis, 1976). Nowhere is this dark side to education seen more clearly than in the outbreak of violent conflict, when education is often used as a tool to promote further violence.

This chapter discusses the complex relationship between education and conflict, and looks at the provision of international education programmes during conflicts, in post-conflict contexts and in other emergencies. It begins by discussing the changing nature of armed conflicts and examines the complex role of education as both a contributing and a mitigating factor in the outbreak of conflict. It then turns to the provision of education in post-conflict contexts, and performs an analysis of the interplay between education and conflict in Nepal's decade long civil war.

Contemporary conflicts and emergencies

Kaldor (1998) uses the term 'new wars' to describe contemporary violent conflicts. Unlike wars of the past, which were generally fought between nation-states over formal political or territorial disputes, new wars are fought within countries' borders over issues of ethnic, linguistic and religious identity. These internal conflicts are increasingly common: 24 active conflicts in 1997 were internal, only one (involving India and Pakistan) was fought between countries (Bush and Saltarelli, 2000). In 2009, all 29 active conflicts were within national borders rather than between them (Heidelberg Institute, 2009). Examples of recent or ongoing internal conflicts include those in Somalia (Moyi, 2012), Darfur in Sudan (Hagan and Kaiser, 2011), Nepal (Shields and Rappleye, 2008b), Peru (Paulson, 2011) and Colombia (Novelli, 2010) and recent violence in Syria and Libya.

While 'old wars' between nation-states (e.g. World Wars I and II) involved horrific acts of mass violence through staged, organized battles, new wars are less structured, often involving guerrilla warfare and battles fought in and around civilian settings (Kaldor, 1998). One consequence of this shift is that children are increasingly involved in conflict, both as victims of violence and, increasingly, as soldiers. A recent UNESCO report estimated that:

> Over 2 million children were killed in conflicts and 6 million disabled in the decade to 2008. Around 300,000 children are being exploited as soldiers, placed on the front line by warring parties. And 20 million children have had to flee their homes as refugees or IDPs. (UNESCO, 2011:142)

Another consequence of new wars is that they reveal 'fault lines' (UNESCO, 2011:162) of division and segregation within societies: because they are fought within national boundaries, the ways in which ethnic, linguistic and religious groups are excluded or marginalized is often manifested in the outbreak of violent conflict. Both these aspects of new wars are relevant to education: education systems have direct contact with a country's children and are also responsible for passing on prejudicial beliefs and practices that exclude and marginalize groups within society. All this underlines that educational policy and practice are increasingly relevant to the outbreak of (and, by extension, the prevention of) violent conflict.

The two faces of education and conflict

If one believes that education is a force for good, then one would also assume that it would generally promote peaceful, democratic societies and reduce the outbreak of violent conflict. However, recent research suggests that such an optimistic view of education is unrealistic. Instead, Buckland argues that 'education systems are almost always complicit in conflict' (Buckland, 2005:85) because they reproduce the inequalities, prejudices, attitudes and beliefs that are at the root of violence. Thus, Bush and Saltarelli (2000) speak of 'two faces' of education and conflict. The first 'face' of education is positive: it can promote social cohesion and integration between different groups within a society and expand the opportunities available to individuals. Schools provide a space to discuss differences and create a society founded on open communication and mutual respect. Curricula can include information on human rights, democracy and citizenship, and pedagogical practices can build mutual respect and tolerance between different ethnic, religious and linguistic groups.

However, according to Bush and Saltarelli (2000) education has a negative face that reproduces inequalities, economic exploitation, racial and ethnic stereotyping and gender divisions. These social evils are often among the root causes of conflict. The negative face is present in many aspects of education – from curriculum to pedagogy to policy, often in ways that are subtle, yet also deeply ingrained and pervasive. For example, curriculum distortion – the selective and biased portrayal of subjects (particularly history, social studies and citizenship) – marginalizes social groups and creates divisions that fuel conflict (Buckland, 2005). One way in which this distortion works is through text books. For example, in the 1980s and 1990s USAID funded new text-books for schools in Afghanistan (Paulson and Rappleye, 2007). In order to bolster opposition to Soviet communist rule, these textbooks were filled with references to warfare: children learned to count, add and subtract using bullets as learning aids (Stephens and Ottaway, 2002). More advanced mathematics problems required students to calculate the speed of bullets and the force of explosives; all students learned how to properly use a Kalashnikov rifle (Off, 2004). These images normalized violence, promoted militant visions of Afghan national identity and Islam and contributed to violent rule under the Taliban and widespread conflict in recent years.

In addition to textbooks and the curriculum, pedagogic practices can also embed overt forms of discrimination against ethnic groups. In Rwanda, Rutayisire (2007) reports how teachers would use examples of killing Tutsis (an ethnic minority group that was subjected to mass violence) in arithmetic lessons, asking students 'If you have twenty Tutsi and you kill five, how many do you have left?' (Rutayisire, 2007:117). Normalizing violence towards the Tutsi minorities created a social environment that favoured conflict, ultimately culminating in genocide through the murder of 800,000 to 1 million ethnic minorities in 1994 (Schweisfurth, 2006).

Policies and practices relating to the language of instruction can be particularly contentious with respect to conflict, with no easy answers for policymakers. For example, Buckland (2005:10) describes how educational policies in Sri Lanka effectively segregated Tamil- and Sinhalese-speaking children, destroying a shared national identity while creating deep divisions and a sense of alienation that fuelled widespread conflict over several decades. However, even standardizing a single language of instruction can be problematic, particularly when it involves the language of a dominant social group being imposed on linguistic minorities. Buckland (2005) also gives the example of how the Serbian language was imposed on students in Kosovo, leading to feelings of oppression and resentment that surfaced in violent conflict throughout the 1990s.

Thus, education is not 'inevitably a force for good' (Bush and Saltarelli, 2000:54); rather, it is potentially a source of great harm and a contributing factor in the outbreak of violent conflict. However, the relationship between education and conflict is more complicated than a two faces analysis suggests, as links between the two continue to be important throughout the course of a conflict.

Beyond two faces: the education and conflict dialectic

As the two faces concept has gained currency as a way of thinking about education and conflict, further research has revealed a more complex and nuanced relationship, showing that lines of influence and causality work in two directions (Paulson, 2008). Just as education can both cause and avert the outbreak of violent conflict, conflict itself has profound effects on education (Davies, 2010). In many cases, violence occurs on or around school grounds, forcing school closures, disrupting education and, in the worst cases, injuring or killing students. Schools can also shape the course of a conflict in a positive way by providing psychosocial support for students, maintaining social cohesion, and providing an environment that promotes constructive dialogue on divisive issues (Davies, 2010). The two-way relationship between education and conflict continues even after fighting itself has ceased: educational reforms are vital in maintaining stability and re-establishing social relations in post-conflict contexts.

Recognizing the barrier that violent conflict poses for the EFA movement, the 2011 UNESCO EFA *Global Monitoring Report* is devoted to the theme of education and armed conflict (UNESCO, 2011). As evidence of the serious effects of conflict on expanding enrolment, the report notes that 42 per cent of the world's 67 million out-of-school children live in conflict-affected countries (UNESCO, 2011:15). Furthermore, UNESCO (2011:133) highlights links between conflict and other development goals, such as child mortality, literacy and gender equality. Thus, the challenge of attaining universal primary enrolment is also increasingly one of addressing the human toll of violent conflict.

According to UNESCO, the problem is not simply that conflict acts as a barrier to education: educational failures also contribute to escalation of the conflict, creating a vicious cycle of education and conflict. As conflict prevents students from enrolment and completion, it creates social instability and fragmentation that further fan the flames of conflict. Students who are not enrolled in school become soldiers, and national governments divert educational funding to military and defence purposes (UNESCO, 2011). In fact, the *Global Monitoring Report* is markedly political in this respect, blaming both development donors and recipient countries and pointing out that six days of global military expenditure would be sufficient to close the EFA funding gap (UNESCO, 2011:3). Due to socio-economic deterioration, even those who have completed formal schooling are left without jobs, resulting in feelings of frustration and disillusionment that are vented in conflict. UNESCO (2011) discusses how educated youth in Sri Lanka and Nigeria provided a source of highly trained soldiers in times of conflict. All this contributes to a 'deadly spiral' (UNESCO, 2011:128) in which conflict impedes access to education, which in turn creates greater levels of exclusion and fuels further conflict.

The two-way relationship between education and conflict is analysed in detail by Davies (2004), who argues that education and conflict are best understood through the lens of complexity theory, the study of systems that are characterized by high levels of interaction and interconnectivity (Morrison, 2002). According to Davies, the behaviour of such systems is characterized by ongoing, two-way feedback and non-linearity, meaning that they are unpredictable and chaotic (Davies, 2005). However, chaos is not 'an absence of order' but rather 'extremely complex information' creating outcomes that are difficult to predict (Davies, 2005:258). This perspective implies that education and conflict are related in many complex ways, but strict, causal descriptions of the education-conflict relationship cannot be formalized in a way that easily establishes prescriptions for policies and practices that apply in all contexts. Rather, every context must be understood as a unique complex system with its own particular properties and dynamics.

Adding another layer to the complex relationship between education and conflict, Novelli and Cardozo (2008) argue for a greater need to understand conflicts in relation to macroscopic geopolitical contexts. They argue that the structure of the global political economy, which creates high levels of global inequality and marginalizes large groups of people, is often a key factor in the outbreak of conflict within national boundaries. For example, many 'internal' conflicts of the past 50 years – such as those fought in Korea, Vietnam and Afghanistan – involved rival Cold War superpowers supporting opposing sides in order to expand their geopolitical influence (Escobar, 1995). However, according to Novelli and Cardozo, much research on conflict and education is characterized by a 'problem-solving approach' that aims to reduce or prevent violence without fully understanding the influence of the systemic factors on the global level or the heterogeneous and often conflicting interests of the 'international community' (Novelli and Cardozo, 2008:481; 484). In any case, the feasibility and fruitfulness of this problem-solving approach is ultimately limited, unless larger geopolitical contexts and power relationships are taken into account.

Thus, recent research on education and conflict (Davies, 2004) has highlighted the complexity of the relationship between the two: education and conflict both influence one another in ways that are complex, non-linear and difficult to predict. Furthermore, although new wars are fought within national boundaries, they are nevertheless significantly affected by larger global relationships. While it is clear that education and conflict are often deeply interlinked, it is difficult to draw far-reaching conclusions that apply across all contexts, particularly in a way that would be useful in preventing or reducing the outbreak of violence. This combination of urgency and ambiguity creates a formidable set of challenges for those planning and implementing education programmes in conflict-affected and post-conflict societies.

Education in emergencies: conflict and post-conflict settings

As research (Bush and Saltarelli, 2000; Davies, 2004) has highlighted that education and conflict are closely linked, it has also established a need for programmes, policies and practices that prevent or reduce violent conflict. The provision of education in conflict-affected societies has coincided with and benefited from a growing interest in providing education in emergencies. In the past, long-term development planning has remained separate and distinct from humanitarian aid programmes, which address acute needs of populations following natural disasters, conflicts, and other rapid-onset emergencies. Development donors such as USAID and the United Nations have created specialized departments that deal with humanitarian aid in emergency situations as separate and distinct from long-term development programmes.[1] While long-term development has focused on human capital, poverty alleviation and economic growth, humanitarian aid has been focused on the 'three pillars' of medical care, shelter and food/water (Sinclair, 2001).

However, in recent years humanitarian aid efforts and long-term development programmes have become more similar in nature. On the one hand, 'chronic crises' – those that last for extended durations or those that are recurring in nature (e.g. conflicts or recurring floods and droughts) – require humanitarian responses that are long-term and increasingly similar to those run by development organizations (INEE, 2004). Similarly, development organizations have recognized that effective provision of humanitarian aid is important in maintaining long-term development (Kagawa, 2005). This convergence of humanitarian aid and development programmes, combined with growing recognition of education as a human right, has led calls to establish education as a 'fourth pillar' of humanitarian aid (Sinclair, 2001).

The arguments that support education in emergencies are substantial: advocates point out that education provides a 'safe space' for children in otherwise hostile environments, that keeping schools open provides a sense of stability and a source of psychosocial support, and that educational settings are an entry point for the provision of other services such as nutrition and healthcare (INEE, 2004). Benefits of education extend to the wider community: schools are able to disseminate 'life-saving information' to students' families, and they help to maintain social cohesion and integration, acting as a barrier to fragmentation and violence (INEE, 2004:2). However, as a component of humanitarian aid, education is relatively marginal. In the 2011 EFA *Global Monitoring Report*, UNESCO points out that education programmes receive less than 2 per cent of overall humanitarian aid funding, and only 38 per cent of education-related funding appeals during emergencies are met by donors, half the average of other sectors such as food and shelter (UNESCO, 2011:3).

Development organizations have responded to the demand for education in emergencies with increased institutional support. In 2000 the Inter-Agency Network for Education in Emergencies (INEE) was founded as a collaborative network of organizations (including donors, NGOs, consultants and international organizations) that provide education in humanitarian emergencies. Through a consultative process, INEE authored its first *Minimum Standards for Education* in 2004, which serves as a guide for organizations providing educational programming in emergency situations. Updated in 2010, INEE's *Minimum Standards* have become a common point of reference for organizations implementing education programmes in emergencies.

However, the field of education in emergencies is not without its perils and criticisms. Bromley and Andina (2010) show that the two faces of education are present even in emergency contexts when 'instead of serving to promote peace and reconciliation', schools become sites for 'further intolerance' (Bromley and Andina, 2010:584). They provide examples of Rwanda, where those responsible for genocide also ran education in refugee camps and Sierra Leone, where girls were denied access to post-conflict education in the name of protection. Novelli and Cardozo also warn that 'the merging of "security" interests with "development" priorities potentially poses dangers to the broader "humanitarian" objectives of aid to education', with the result that 'many NGOs are increasingly concerned that they are becoming adjuncts and auxiliaries to the military adventures of the major Western Powers' (Novelli and Cardozo, 2008:483–4). Thus, even when education is aimed at providing stability in post-conflict contexts, there is still a strong need to critically scrutinize its relationship to conflict.

Reflective Exercise

- Is education a vital aspect of humanitarian relief? If so, should it receive equal funding to other aspects of relief work? What if this came at the expense of funds for food, shelter or medical aid?

Case study: education and conflict in Nepal

The complex relationship between education and conflict can be seen in the decade-long conflict that took place in Nepal between 1996 and 2006. The conflict started when a group of Maoist rebels in a remote part of the country declared a 'People's War' against the government, which at the time was a constitutional monarchy. The situation was worsened when a royal massacre in 2001 created instability in the national government; the new king disbanded parliament in 2002 and eventually declared absolute rule in 2005. It was not until an alliance between Maoists and the disbanded parliament led to mass protests in 2006 that the king was overthrown and a new government formed (Shields and Rappleye, 2008b). However, the post-conflict environment has remained highly unstable (Pherali, 2011). Although Maoists had a strong showing in elections to the constituent assembly, they have remained at odds with more mainstream political parties and the threat of a return to violence is omnipresent.

Education was very much at the heart of the People's War. Among the Maoists' grievances were the right to education in students' mother tongue (rather than the national Nepali language) and the closure of private schools, which the Maoists claimed created a two-tier education system that benefited the wealthy. However, the links between education and conflict ran more deeply than the Maoists' stated demands: for decades the curriculum had promoted a strong vision of national identity centred on conservative visions of

Hinduism and the use of the Nepali language (Shields and Rappleye, 2008a). Pigg (1992) describes how textbooks promoted integration of the country's many diverse ethnic groups in order to create a cohesive national identity, yet in doing so they favoured certain groups as being superior to others. High-caste Hindus – who generally speak the national Nepali language – were depicted in prominent positions in textbook illustrations while ethnic, linguistic and religious minorities were portrayed as deficient, often in the background (Pigg, 1992). This portrayal effectively marginalized many of the country's ethnic and religious minorities, leading to feelings of alienation and antagonism towards the national government. In addition to practices within the classroom, half a century of rapid educational expansion had ingrained into popular consciousness the notion that education would lead to national development and improved standards of living. Although enrolment increased significantly, the promised improvements in employment and income never materialized for much of population. Instead, educated, unemployed, youth provided an ideal body of recruits for the Maoists' People's Army (Shields and Rappleye, 2008b).

During the conflict, schools were heavily politicized and subjected to ideological and physical attacks from both sides. As many remote areas of the country lacked other government offices or infrastructure, schools were the only state-run institution, which meant that 'an attack on the school' was equivalent to 'a symbolic attack on the state itself' (Caddell, 2002:232). Maoists also used schools as a platform to promote their political ideology and to recruit young soldiers for their army (Parker and Standing, 2007). Thus, it is not surprising that on several occasions, fighting between the two sides spilled onto school grounds (Shields and Rappleye, 2008b). Teachers were put into a particularly difficult role, negotiating between the demands of government, the Maoist army, and the communities in which they lived (Shields, 2005). Writing during the conflict, Thapa and Sijipati describe how

> teaching is a risky job in areas where the Maoists are strong. Teachers are at the receiving end from both sides. As people living in Maoist areas, they are viewed with suspicion by the authorities, whilst their regular contacts with the district administration causes them to be viewed with equal distrust by the Maoists. A disproportionate number of teachers have been killed in the conflict. (Thapa and Sijapati, 2004:6)

Nepal's recent history provides an excellent example of how conflict and education are deeply intertwined. It also suggests that this link does not stop at education but rather extends to the larger project of national development in which it is situated. Tracing the origins of the Maoist movement, Rappleye (2011a) describes how a USAID-funded programme in the Maoists' stronghold in the remote west of the country increased the production of cash crops that were sold in India. While the programme benefited large-scale industrial agriculture, it left many of the region's small-scale farmers behind. This was complemented by an educational paradigm centred on the values of 'modernity', including the belief that individual investments in education would inevitably lead to increased opportunities and national development (Pherali, 2011). Carney and Rappleye (2011) link these phenomena in their argument that 'Nepal's experience of modernity through "development", at least as this has manifested in and around the classroom, has contributed directly to the country's devastating civil war' (Carney and Rappleye, 2011:2).

The timeframe of Nepal's conflict also overlaps with a growth in education in emergency programmes. In 2002, a number of development organizations initiated the 'Children as Zones of Peace Programme', which sought to mitigate the effects of conflict, including violence against children and the recruitment of child soldiers, through a programme of peace education and advocacy for children's rights (Parker and Standing, 2007). Even in the post-conflict scenario, education remains a highly politicized and divisive issue, which contributes to a larger context of instability and national fragility (Pherali, 2011).

Using Nepal as a case study, one sees how the education-conflict relationship is complex and multifaceted. While enrolment had expanded greatly over a period of several decades, education contributed to the outbreak of the conflict by reproducing prejudices and marginalizing minority groups. Furthermore, the larger project of national development in which educational expansion was situated was exclusionary, benefiting some while leaving others behind. Throughout the conflict, schools were severely affected by the conflict as violence targeted both teachers and students.

Reflective Exercise

- Do you think that policymakers in Nepal could have averted the conflict through educational reform? Is there any way they could have foreseen the outbreak of conflict?

Summary

This chapter has shown that education and violent conflict are often deeply interlinked. While this relationship is complex, two-way and unpredictable, it is clear that education is not always a force for good. Rather, education has two faces in relation to conflict: on one hand it mitigates and prevents conflict by promoting dialogue and social cohesion. On the other hand, education reproduces social inequalities and prejudice, which often fuel and exacerbate the outbreak of violence. Growing awareness into the close connection between education and conflict has led to increased provision of education programmes as a way to promote cohesion and avert violence in conflict-affected societies. This contributes to and benefits from a wider movement towards education in emergencies, the integration of educational components in humanitarian aid and relief.

Education in conflicts and emergencies is an emerging field, and one that is unique in that it utilizes the institutional apparatuses of development aid (i.e. international organizations, bilateral donors and NGOs) in a way that is separate and distinct from international development. Rather than a long-term vision of social and economic progress, the focus is on immediate needs and maintaining social stability. This move away from relatively simple, linear notions of development is representative of the larger recognition of the increasing complexity of education in global contexts, which is explored in the following chapter.

Reflective Exercise

- If education is not 'inevitably a force for good' (Bush and Saltarelli, 2000:54), but also a contributing factor in the outbreak of conflict, does that mean that the 2015 target of EFA should be reconsidered or delayed? Are there contexts in which expanding access to education might not be a good idea? If so when, and why?

Useful websites

http://blogs.worldbank.org/conflict/ – World Bank blogs relating to conflict and development. Last accessed on 4 May 2012.

http://oneresponse.info/GlobalClusters/Education/ – The United Nations education cluster for humanitarian disaster response. Last accessed on 4 May 2012.

www.ineesite.org/ – The Inter-Agency Network for Education in Emergencies. Last accessed on 4 May 2012.

Note

1   For USAID, this is the Office of Foreign Disaster Assistance (OFDA); for the United Nations it is the Office for the Coordination of Humanitarian Affairs (OCHA).

Conceptualizing Globalization and Education

5

Introduction

Giddens (1999:7) declares 'For better or worse, we are being propelled into a global order that no one fully understands, but which is making its effects felt upon all of us'. This claim succinctly articulates much of the uncertainty and change associated with globalization, but his wording suggests that this process is unmediated and inevitable. One might rightly question whether 'we are being propelled' into this new global order, or, actually, some group is actively 'propelling us' to serve its interests.

This chapter examines the complex phenomenon of globalization and analyses its importance for the study of education. It begins by discussing the term 'globalization' itself, showing how its meaning is variable and contested and then looks at how globalization challenges the assumptions upon which the field of comparative and international education is built (see Chapter 1). After this, it discusses theoretical perspectives on *why* and *how* globalization is occurring and looks at the decentralization of education as a case study of globalization in action.

The globalization perspective

The term globalization has become widely used in nearly all walks of life, including not only academic research, but also popular media, private businesses and non-profit organizations. However, for this very reason its meaning is unclear: globalization means many things to many people, and in some senses the term has come to mean less as its use has become widespread (Sklair, 1999). Much of this ambiguity can be attributed to the complex and multifaceted nature of globalization: it is not a unitary process or force, but rather a set of interrelated changes. Among these are increased international flows of money, goods, people, ideas, information and communication (DFID, 2000); a social convergence on common cultural values, social practices, economic structures and governance (Meyer et al., 1997); and an increase in social and political processes that occur 'above' the level of the nation-states and their governments, mainly through international organizations (e.g. the United Nations, World Bank and World Trade Organization – Spring, 2008).

The origins of the term are found in the field of international economics in the 1960s, referring to increasing international flows of trade and finance (Feder, 2006). Since then, it has been applied to a wide range of topics, and forms a core research theme in fields such as anthropology, sociology and education. In that time, the concept of globalization has gone from a glimpse of an emerging future to a firmly established reality of the present. While it may seem surprising that research has not 'moved on' in other directions, this continued preoccupation with globalization is evidence of its profound importance, and as long as globalization continues to define so many aspects of social life, it will remain a focus of social research.

In the field of education, globalization is most apparent in the convergence of education systems around a common 'international model' of policies and practices (Stener-Khamsi, 2004b). This is sometimes referred to as isomorphism (Meyer et al., 1997), from the Greek roots *iso* (meaning 'same') and *morph* (meaning 'shape'). For example, every government in the world provides education to its citizens; this education system is coordinated by a central ministry of education and delivered through a system of schools. Internally, schools are all organized into classrooms that are led by certified professional teachers. Students study a standard curriculum that varies little according to their own national and cultural context; as Meyer et al. (1997:149–50) point out, .

> Children who will become agricultural laborers study fractions; villagers in remote regions learn about chemical reactions, members of marginalized groups who will never see a ballot box study their national constitution.

Furthermore, education systems change in similar ways at similar times. For example, many countries (e.g. the United Kingdom – see Gove, 2010) are currently increasing performance benchmarking (using standardized tests to assess school performance), looking to market-based policies, and advocating an increased role for private schools.

Reflective Exercise

- What images does the term globalization bring to mind? Does it have positive or negative connotations?

The challenge to comparative education

Previous chapters have shown that international initiatives in education (e.g. as part of international aid and development) existed decades before anyone was discussing globalization and education. With this in mind, it is apt to question whether globalization is really a new phenomenon, or simply a new 'twist' on trends that have been ongoing for quite some time. In fact, there is truth to both of these positions; globalization is a continuation of long-standing trends towards international integration, but a key claim of research on the topic is that the current era of globalization is discontinuous with and qualitatively different from the world order that preceded it (Clayton, 2004; Sklair, 1999). This is certainly true with respect to the field of comparative and international education (see Introduction): many of the topics that are now discussed in relation to globalization and education (e.g. the borrowing and lending of policies, student achievement, literacy and enrolment) had been studied for quite some time in the field of comparative education before the study of globalization existed. However, the perspective of globalization also represents a fundamentally new perspective on the international study of education, and challenges the foundations of the field of comparative education in several respects.

First, globalization entails that many aspects of a country's educational policies are not determined by its national government, but rather by the declarations and commitments of international organizations. In the words of Spring (2008:1), 'The image is that of global educational policies and practices existing in a superstructure above national and local schools'. The Education for All (EFA) movement (Chapter 3) is one such example of a policy that originates in this global superstructure: The World Conference on Education for All (1990) was initiated by a number of international organizations, and by signing the Jomtien Declaration virtually every country in the world has committed to providing free, compulsory education to all its citizens. Whether it meets their own priorities, national governments have little real choice in committing to EFA: by refusing to do so they would be condemned as cruel dictatorships that deprive their population of basic human rights. This challenges approaches to international education that focus primarily on the nation-state: if national governments are no longer truly responsible for setting their educational policies, then analysis must look above and beyond the national level to find the true agents of educational change. Comparisons on the level of the nation-state provide little insight into these 'supernational' (or global) aspects of policy making.

Second, comparative education relies upon the notion of distinct, separate societies that can be juxtaposed with one another. Research in the field has used the nation-state as the unit of analysis, treating national boundaries as the 'the container of social and political life' (Robertson, 2011:2). For this reason, comparative studies in international education have tended to emphasize differences between countries: for example they compare differences in enrolment, literacy and achievement between two or more countries (Phillips and Schweisfurth, 2008). These differences are then attributed to features of the national context (i.e. culture, geography and history) and used to explain its level of socio-economic development. Ultimately, practice in the field of international education and development suggests that changes in national governance can ostensibly improve education and standard of living for the entire country. However, this approach begins with the assumption that the nation-state can be treated as an isolated unit without considering the context of global relations in which it is embedded, but globalization challenges the notion that such clear boundaries exist.

Third, the globalization perspective takes a more nuanced and complex view of inequalities than comparative international studies. By using the nation-state as the unit of analysis, international comparisons concentrate on inequalities *between* countries – for example UNDP's annual *Human Development Report* ranks every country in the world on its level of socio-economic development (UNDP, 2010). What this approach ignores are the very large inequalities that exist *within* countries – for example differences in income between the rich and poor, or gaps in educational quality between urban and rural areas. Arguably, these internal inequalities are far greater than those between countries (Sen, 1999). For example, low-income individuals in the United States may have much in common with low-income individuals in other countries (e.g. India): in both countries the poor can rarely afford to own their own home and have trouble accessing education and healthcare (Deaton and Kozel, 2005; DeVoe et al., 2007). Similarly, India's middle class is increasingly similar to that in the United States, consuming the same brands of food and clothing (Ablett et al., 2007), working for the same multinational companies, and even sending their children to the same universities (see Chapter 8). In contrast, high- and low-income individuals in each country may share little in common, and may not even speak the same language. As inequalities cut across national boundaries, it makes little sense to speak of education in India or the United States as a homogenous entity. The globalization perspective acknowledges this complexity and examines inequalities both within and between countries.

Theoretical perspectives on globalization

A great deal of discussion on globalization focuses on its effects, rather than its processes (Beckfield, 2010; Robertson, Bonal and Dale, 2002). For example, it is common to question whether the spread of global media is causing a loss of local culture (Tomlinson, 2000), or whether the rise of transnational corporations and international organizations undermines small businesses and national governments (Stiglitz, 2002; Giddens, 1999). It has even been suggested that globalization underlies a 'clash of civilizations' between the Christian 'West' and Muslim 'East' (Huntington, 1997). However, such questions ignore the important question *why* globalization is causing such unprecedented changes.

The intertwined questions of 'why' and 'how' globalization occurs are addressed in several theoretical conceptualizations of globalization discussed in this section (Sklair, 1999). These perspectives have much in common: all acknowledge that one change associated with globalization is that countries and their education systems have become isomorphic: governments share similar structures, with nationally elected parliaments, ministerial structures and local governing bodies. Every country provides state-sponsored education that is compulsory, governed by a central ministry or department of education, and delivered in schools by trained, certified teaching professionals. However, these perspectives give very different reasons for the underlying causes of this isomorphism and the underlying nature of globalization.

Globalization as competition: neoliberalism

American journalist Thomas Friedman (2000:14) claims that globalization is creating an 'integration of markets, nation-states and technologies to a degree never witnessed before – in a way that is enabling individuals, corporations and nation-states to reach round the world farther, faster, deeper and cheaper than ever before'. These views emphasize the competitive nature of globalization, which is articulated in the economic school of thought known as neoliberalism. Neoliberalism holds that the competitive forces of the market are beneficial: as individuals and businesses compete with one another they adopt practices that are more innovative and efficient. These ideas date back to Adam Smith's (1776/1999) concept of the 'invisible hand' of market forces, the notion that through competition with one another economic rivals are naturally guided towards greater efficiency, better products and higher levels of innovation.

In the neoliberal perspective, the key element of globalization is a removal of barriers to international competition. For example, free trade agreements have reduced import/export taxes and increased international trade; the internet has allowed the free flow of information and communication throughout most of the world; reduced restrictions on visas have increased international travel and migration. Neoliberalism (Tooley, 1997) argues that these changes are good: competition creates efficiency and economic growth and spurs technological innovation, all of which ultimately improve the lives of individuals. Furthermore, neoliberalism claims that open global competition increases opportunities for billions of talented workers around the world: Friedman (2006) claims that globalization is creating a 'flat world' that is more fair and equitable; an individual's achievements are determined by his or her hard work and abilities rather than country of birth.

However, these changes also create challenges and instability. Multinational corporations are able to relocate jobs to virtually any country in which they can be performed at the lowest cost. This means that individuals face constant uncertainty in their employment. Through networks of global finance, these corporations can also 'offshore' their profits to reduce the amount of tax they pay, meaning that governments are less able to rely on tax revenues (Giddens, 1999). The position of national governments is further weakened by the increased power of international organizations and their binding declarations, which constrain the range of policy options open to them and commit them to global free trade (Verger, 2009). The net result is that the lives of individuals are less certain, and national governments are less able to offer the comprehensive social security 'safety net' that they provided in the past (Giddens, 1999). Despite these downsides, neoliberalism argues that globalization is largely inevitable, and individual nations that attempt to resist it would face isolation and even greater levels of insecurity.

Competition theories (Friedman, 2000) explain the convergence of education systems as gravitation towards 'best practices': as countries compete with one another in the global economy, they are likely to adopt whatever policies and practices are most effective. Thus, education systems come to resemble one another as they are guided by the 'invisible hand' of market forces to similar practices and policies. While nation-states and international organizations play an important role in facilitating this convergence, their actual agency is rather limited and reflects the 'common sense' understanding that universal, efficient, high-quality education is necessary in a competitive society.

Globalization as conflict: world systems analysis

While neoliberalism might accept that globalization is an inevitable outcome of competitive market forces, conflict perspectives are more cautious and critical, examining ways in which the changes caused by globalization tend to benefit those who are already most powerful (Spring, 2008). Conflict perspectives reject Friedman's (2006) claim that globalization is creating a flat world, instead arguing that globalization is actively promoted by global elites (i.e. rich and powerful individuals and institutions) to further entrench and perpetuate their advantage. Since it is an active attempt by one group to increase its power, this notion implicitly rejects the idea that globalization is an inevitable process that cannot or should not be resisted. In reality, the discourse of inevitability is one form of ideological manipulation used by elites to further their own interests.

The strongest articulation of conflict perspectives on globalization is found in world systems analysis, a theoretical perspective developed by sociologist Immanuel Wallerstein in his three-volume manuscript *The Modern World System* (Wallerstein, 1974). In short, world systems analysis argues that the global economy has become so closely knit that it makes sense to speak of a single integrated world economic system. However, this world economic system is characterized by an unequal core/periphery relationship: a relatively small number of core countries have large amounts of capital, higher incomes, and are in an advantageous position in world trade. In contrast, a much larger group of countries form the periphery, which is economically dependent on the core (Arnove, 2009). The relationship between the core and periphery is somewhat akin to the Marxist concept of the class struggle between capital owners (*bourgeoisie*) and the working class (*proletariat*): the working class (or global periphery) is economically dependent upon the capital owners (or the global core), but because the former outnumber the latter significantly, they are unable to negotiate a more equitable relationship, and so the state of dependence perpetuates.

In explaining the convergence of education systems around a common set of policies and practices, world systems analysis looks to the strong influence that core countries are able to exert in the periphery. While national governments engage in diplomacy bilaterally and through international organizations, this is essentially a façade (what is called the 'superstruture' in Marxist analyses) that perpetuates relationships of domination (Clayton, 2004). What is often described as global policy-making is, in fact, the agenda of powerful actors in the world economic system: national governments of 'core' countries acting in the interests of capital owners. This agenda is enacted through an 'international network of aid and knowledge diffusion' (Arnove, 1980:51), including the World Bank, United Nations, bilateral donors, and philanthropic foundations (e.g. the Bill and Melinda Gates Foundation, 2009). This network claims to work towards goals of poverty reduction, development and education for all, but in doing so it also perpetuates existing power relations and maintains the core/periphery structure of the international economic system. Education plays a large part in this process: it prepares the future workforce of the global economic system. In many cases this involves uprooting or eliminating elements of traditional cultures that are not integrated into the world economy and spreading values of capitalism, consumerism and rational economic behaviour. The net result is that education systems become increasingly similar, but this similarity is rooted in global relationships that are fundamentally characterized by the dominance of one powerful group (i.e. the core) over the less-powerful (i.e. the periphery), a form of oppression and control commonly referred to as 'hegemony' (Hill, 2007).

Globalization as culture: world culture theory

In contrast to conflict and competition theories, world culture theory (also called neo-institutionalism or world polity theory) views globalization primarily as a diffusion of cultural values. These values include democratic citizenship, respect for individual rights, rational decision making and autonomy and self-determination of the individual (Boli and Thomas, 1997). They are embodied in the declarations of international organizations (e.g. the UN Declaration of Human Rights), and imported to the national contexts through the national policies of individual countries that constitute the membership of these organizations (Meyer et al., 1997). As globalization spreads, these values are regarded less as culturally specific (i.e. elements of Western European societies) and more as universal truths that are applicable worldwide.

To illustrate this case, world culture theorists pose an interesting hypothetical question. 'If an unknown society were "discovered" on a previously unknown island' what changes would occur? (Meyer et al., 1997:145). They answer that a series of transformations to the island society can be predicted. Rather than being conquered or colonized by another country (as it might have been, several hundred years ago), the island would come to form an independent, sovereign nation-state, regarded as equal to other nation-states. It would have a government with a similar structure to that of other countries, with ministries of trade, health and education. The island would join international organizations such as the United Nations, and would commit to their declarations and conventions – for example the Universal Declaration of Human Rights (United Nations, 1948) and the World Declaration of Education for All (World Conference on Education for All, 1990). If preexisting practices on the island were contrary to world culture values (if, for example, it practised child labour, overt discrimination, dictatorial rule), those practices would be eventually considered illegitimate and banned. Over time, citizens of the island would come to accept notions of progress and development associated with 'Western' modernity (Meyer et al., 1997).

The hypothetical case of the island demonstrates key aspects of world culture theory. First, world culture theory claims that international organizations are key agents of globalization: through their declarations and commitments these institutions establish and disseminate the values of world culture. Second, because nation-states constitute the membership of these international organizations, world culture theory argues that they become stronger, not weaker, as a result of globalization. In this respect it differs considerably from neoliberalism, which claims that globalization undermines the nation-state by removing its protective barriers and political autonomy. Third, world culture theory argues that most of the changes associated with globalization are caused by shifts in underlying cultural values, not by the economic factors or functional considerations that are often given as justifications. For example, world culture theory rejects 'conventional legitimations for mass schooling' that 'insist that formal education is necessary and beneficial for economic growth, technical innovation, citizen loyalty, and democratic institutions' and instead posit cultural changes as the primary reason for the expansion of mass education throughout the world (Meyer et al., 1997:149). Finally, world culture theory differs from conflict theories in that it claims that these cultural changes are 'surprisingly consensual', and, therefore, are not the result of hegemonic power relationships such as those described by world systems analysis.

World culture theory ascribes a very central role to education: it is one of the primary transmitters of world culture, and the spread of schooling throughout the twentieth century was largely correlated with the spread of international organizations (Benavot and Riddle, 1988; Boli, Ramirez and Meyer, 1985). However, world culture theory rejects the functional rationalization of education as human capital (Meyer et al., 1997). Instead, it claims that the convergence of education systems worldwide is caused by the spread of world culture values, particularly the notion that individuals have the right to education, and that personal, rational knowledge is valuable. International organizations play a key role in the spread of these values – for instance the role of UNESCO and the World Bank in the EFA movement has extended access to primary education to many children. However, unlike world systems analysis, world culture theory describes this process as 'surprisingly consensual' (Meyer et al, 1997:145); international organizations do not serve the interests of global elites but rather reflect a broad agreement between member states.

Reflective exercise

Schooling is arguably the most global institution in the world. Schools can be found in virtually every country, and every government provides education to its citizens. Despite vast differences in countries' histories, languages, cultures and economies, schooling is always done in very much the same way: trained teachers work in classrooms to deliver a curriculum divided into the same subjects. Why has education become standardized in this way around the world? Was it through force or consensus? Is this form of schooling the best model of education for all societies?

Case study: globalization and decentralization

Nothing better illustrates the globalization of education than the ongoing trend towards the decentralization of education in many countries. From Argentina to Zambia, national governments are reducing their involvement in education and looking to local communities, the private sector and charitable organizations to play a greater role in the operation of schools (Bray, 1996; Rhoten, 2000). This is truly a global phenomenon; decentralization initiatives have become so widespread that they have been called a 'mantra that is recited regardless of the circumstances of specific settings' (Mullikottu-Veettil and Bray, 2004:224).

Decentralization has received considerable support from international organizations and from bilateral aid donors (see Chapter 2). Since the early 1980s, the World Bank has supported decentralization initiatives in official policy documents and reports, a position which USAID and UNESCO began to support in the 1990s (Rhoten, 2000: 601–2). Support for decentralization is underpinned by several interrelated arguments. First, proponents of decentralization claim that it increases efficiency; decentralization frees schools from the bureaucracy of central government and adherence to regulations that may not be relevant in local contexts (Lai-ngok, 2004). Second, supporters claim that decentralization empowers parents, teachers and local communities by allowing them to take a more active role in the management of schools; these groups are transformed from passive recipients of a state service into active participants in delivering education. Because members of the community are involved in governance and management, schools also become more accountable to their local communities (Carney and Bista, 2009). Finally, decentralization is seen to open new doors for school financing through the involvement of local businesses and charitable organizations (Astiz, Wiseman and Baker, 2002). However, all of these cases for decentralization share a common set of assumptions: the national government is seen as inefficient, unresponsive, heavy-handed and non-participatory, and its involvement as undesirable. The solution to these shortcomings is to minimize state involvement in education (Carney, 2009).

However, the implementation of decentralization measures in national contexts varies considerably. For instance, in the United States the decentralization of education has been furthered through the establishment of charter schools, which are funded by the government but are autonomous from local educational governance and have greater control over staffing, curriculum and teaching practices (Carnoy et al., 2009). In return, charter schools provide accountability, committing to achieve certain performance standards. Charter schools are similar to academies in the United Kingdom, which are also publicly funded and teach the National Curriculum, but are governed and partly funded by local businesses and charitable organizations (Gunter, 2011). In a similar vein, the World Bank sponsored implementation of community managed schooling in El Salvador, Tanzania and Nepal reduces oversight from the Ministry of Education by establishing local school management committees, which have substantial power in running the school, and are supposed to address problems of teacher absenteeism, poor quality and a purported lack of support from the central government (Carney and Bista, 2009; Miller-Grandvaux, 2002; Jiminez and Sawada, 1998).

Each of the theoretical perspectives discussed above (section 3) acknowledges that decentralization exemplifies the convergence of educational policies in many countries around an 'international model' (Steiner-Khamsi, 2004b:3). However, these theories provide very different accounts of why this convergence is occurring. From a neoliberal standpoint, the trend towards decentralization is easily explained as the emergence of a 'best practice': as globalization puts countries in greater competition with one another, there is more pressure on education systems to perform efficiently (Burde, 2004). Neoliberalism claims that decentralization increases accountability, which improves the efficiency of education. Therefore, the common trend towards decentralization is easily explained as a result of the increased competitive pressures of globalization. Because these competitive pressures are the same in all countries throughout the world, it is expected that countries would respond in similar ways, explaining why the move towards decentralization is so prevalent. Rhoten (2000:594) notes that decentralization initiatives are underpinned by the assumption that the welfare state (i.e. national governments that provide high levels of social services) is no longer feasible in an age of intense economic globalization. This conforms to the neoliberal expectation that globalization usurps the role of the nation-state, the only way that national governments can expect to survive is to look for new ways to deliver social services (including education) effectively.

In contrast, world systems analysis points out that neoliberalism completely ignores the intense power struggles involved in decentralization. Furthermore, the world systems perspective claims that decentralization initiatives tend to benefit elites (i.e. those in situations of greater economic or political power) at both the national and the local levels. The ways in which it does so are manifold and complex: for example, elites may use decentralization initiatives to increase their influence in school policy making by joining school management boards (Edwards, 2011), to divert resources towards 'high performing' schools in affluent areas, or to increase the presence of private schools (Carney and Bista, 2009). The trend towards decentralization can, therefore, be explained by the common interests of elites around the world: acting both through international organizations (i.e. the World Bank) and at the local level (e.g. on school management committees). This is supported by an ideological rhetoric about increased efficiency and accountability, but this is inaccurate and disingenuous. The real driving forces behind decentralization, claim conflict theorists, are power relations.

Conflict theories do not view the nation-state as fundamentally under-mined by globalization, as neoliberalism does, but they point out the clear hierarchy that exists in global policy making. For example, Carney and Bista's (2009) anthropological study of decentralization in Nepal shows that policy making in the Ministry of Education is effectively dictated by the World Bank, which primarily acts in the interests of global elites. The Ministry of Education, and with it the nation-state, are necessary in facilitating and pro-viding legitimacy for this transfer, but it lacks agency and is fundamentally disempowered.

Finally, world culture theory explains the global trend towards decen-tralization as an expression of world culture ideals of autonomy, individual-ism, accountability and citizenship (Boli and Thomas, 1997), which entail that schools should be run democratically by stakeholders. These values are embodied in international organizations, which express their support for decentralization expressed in official documents (e.g. Barrera-Osorio et al., 2009; Lugaz and De Grauwe, 2010). National governments and their ministries of education then adopt these 'policy scripts', importing world culture values and ideals into their national context (Astiz, Wiseman and Baker, 2002). This diffusion to national contexts is an important part of world culture theory, and for this reason it rejects the neoliberal claim that the nation-state is effectively undermined by decentralization policies and the larger processes of globalization in which it is situated. On the contrary, national governments are key actors in implementing the global policy scripts within local contexts. Additionally, world culture theory emphasizes that this process is driven by diplomacy and consensus among states that are sovereign equals, implicitly negating the world systems' emphasis on power and hegemony.

Clearly, each of these theories has some validity. The neoliberal perspec-tive is supported by increased competition between schools and the pres-sures for reform that this creates. However world systems theorists would rightly point out that this increased competition takes place in the context of wider relationships of conflict and hegemony, and powerful groups are able to use autonomy to further their own advantage by influencing school management. Similarly, international institutions have a clear influence over policy and practice, as predicted by world culture theory (Astiz, Wiseman and Baker, 2002). Thus, all theories have some validity, yet none offers a com-plete account of the dynamics involved in globalization.

Summary

This chapter has examined globalization and the many ways in which it is affecting education around the world. The origins of the term 'globalization' are found in the field of international economics, but the concept has been applied to virtually all social science disciplines. Globalization has come to mean different things to different groups of people; in fact it is such a variable concept that in many senses it lacks a concrete meaning. The study of globalization and education differs from international comparative studies in several important respects: the globalization perspective acknowledges that significant educational policy decisions are taken at the supranational (or global) level, and growing inequalities within countries and similarities between countries render many national comparisons meaningless.

The chapter examined three dominant theories of globalization from a broad base of social science literature: neoliberalism, world systems analysis, and world culture theory. The first of these views globalization primarily as a phenomenon of increased competition; as countries compete with one another in the global economy they become more similar in many ways, including their education systems. In contrast, world systems analysis attributes growing similarities in education systems to global power relations and the influence of elites. Finally, world culture theory identifies international organizations such as the World Bank and United Nations as key agents of globalization: through their international declarations these organizations embody a 'world culture' that values individualism, democracy and human rights. These competing theoretical conceptualizations all acknowledge increased similarities in education systems, such as the trend towards decentralization, but they offer very different accounts for why it is happening.

This chapter underlines that globalization is surrounded by controversy and confusion. There is disagreement over what the term itself means, heated debate about whether it is for the better or for the worse, and competing theoretical conceptualizations about how and why globalization occurs. An unexpected outcome is that in the midst of this confusion and disagreement there is remarkable clarity on key issues and questions for research. Regardless of their theoretical position, researchers are asking why education systems throughout the world are converging on a common set of policies and practices, examining the effects of international organizations in contributing to this isomorphism, and questioning the future of the nation-state in a globalized world.

Reflective Exercise

Meyer et al. (1997) ask 'If an unknown society were "discovered" on a previously unknown island' what changes would occur? They predict that the following would happen:

- the island society would become a nation-state, with a government like other nation-states
- it would join international organizations, beginning with the United Nations
- international organizations would collect data about the society, which would be used to plan its development
- the island's government would provide education and other services to its people
- the concepts of progress and development would take hold.

Do you agree with this? If not, what do you think would happen differently? Is there anything they have missed? What do the changes to this hypothetical island society say about the processes of globalization?

Useful websites

http://infed.org/features/globalization_feature.htm – Globalization and education at the Informal Education Encyclopaedia (Infed). Last accessed on 4 May 2012.

http://video.mit.edu/watch/the-world-is-flat-30-9321 – Journalist Thomas Friedman speaking of the 'flat world' view of globalization. Last accessed on 4 May 2012.

Education and the Global Knowledge Economy

6

Chapter Outline

Introduction

The role of knowledge and information has become increasingly important in the lives of people around the world. Examples of this abound: more than a billion people use the internet to find information and communicate with one another (Economist, 2009), while emerging fields of science and engineering such as nanotechnology rely heavily on the continuing creation and application of new knowledge. Recognizing a rise in economic activity centred on the exchange of knowledge and information, Drucker (1968) claimed that societies were shifting to a 'knowledge economy', in which knowledge is transformed into 'intellectual property' that is produced, exchanged, sold and consumed.

This chapter discusses the concept of the global knowledge economy and what it means for education. It begins by defining the global knowledge economy, tracing the origins of the concept and how it has gained currency conceptualization of education's role in society. The next section looks at examples of how knowledge economy discourses have shaped education policy and practice, with special attention to the increasing importance placed on international achievement tests, standardized exams given to students in many countries in order to measure and compare academic achievement. Finally, the chapter offers critical perspectives on the knowledge economy.

Conceptualizing the global knowledge economy

The growth of industrialization throughout the eighteenth and nineteenth century was based on a continuous cycle of capitalist production in which raw materials (e.g. cotton, wood or copper) and labour are used to create manufactured products (e.g. clothing, furniture or electronics) that are sold at a profit. This profit is then reinvested to acquire further raw materials and labour, and the cycle continues (Jessop, 2002). Through colonial conquest, this cycle of capitalist production became global in scope: raw materials were exported from colonized countries (e.g. cotton from India), transformed into finished products in European factories, and re-exported worldwide (although the profits remained largely in Europe – Wallerstein, 1974; Pratt-Adams et al., 2010).

However, by the latter half of the twentieth century, the role of specialized technical knowledge became increasingly important in capitalist production, as advances in technology increased the efficiency of manufacturing, requiring less labour input and thereby increasing end profits (Gürüz, 2008). Furthermore, developments in physical sciences and engineering offered opportunities to develop new products and even new industries (e.g. computer hardware and software, mobile phone and wireless technologies, pharmaceuticals). The ability to capitalize on these opportunities required a quick transformation from scientific discovery to technological innovation to marketable product, which was only possible with a highly skilled workforce. Thus, in a short time technical knowledge became valued as a commodity in its own right.

Recognizing this trend, in 1968 Peter Drucker used the term 'knowledge economy' to describe economic activity that centres primarily on the exchange of knowledge, ideas and information rather than raw materials and manufactured goods (Drucker, 1968). According to Drucker, the knowledge economy required a new labour force of 'knowledge workers', who were paid based on their ability to think, analyse and innovate rather than to perform a predefined set of tasks. Writing at roughly the same time, Daniel Bell (1973) described the coming of a 'post-industrial' society, referring to the shift away from capitalist industrial economics towards a new paradigm in which science and knowledge would drive economic growth. According to Philip Brown and Hugh Lauder, (2006:26) in this new economic order 'it is no longer ownership of capital that generates wealth creation but the application of knowledge'.

Drucker (1968) and Bell (1973) were writing at the beginning of a rapid growth in knowledge-intensive industries, those in which the value of products and services derives primarily from the knowledge used to create them. Examples of such industries range from computer software to medical research to financial services; the 'knowledge' aspect is not related to the nature of the industry, but to the fact that it is the production of knowledge that creates economic value. In many cases, the end products are not entirely knowledge-based, for example a pharmaceutical company must physically manufacture medicines in order to be financially viable, and computer software companies will often distribute their products on digital media (e.g. CD-ROMs). However, in both cases an item's economic value primarily derives from the knowledge required to produce it rather than from the physical properties of the item itself.

This growth of the knowledge economy was facilitated by several factors: first, larger processes of economic, social and political globalization created a context in which trade and finance flowed more freely across international borders than at any other time in the past. Furthermore, at both the national and international levels, laws around intellectual property have been strengthened, meaning companies that create intellectual property are able to sell their 'products' around the world with relatively little fear of copyright infringement or 'piracy' (Correa, 2001). This has been facilitated by the World Trade Organization's (WTO) 1994 Agreement on Trade-Related Aspects of Intellectual Property Rights (TRIPS), which standardized the rights of patent holders among member countries (Correa, 2001). Finally, the expansion of the knowledge economy has been deeply intertwined with a revolution in information and communications technologies (ICT), particularly the internet, that has made it possible to transmit information around the world instantaneously. This ICT revolution has given the knowledge economy global reach;

through the internet 'knowledge work' can now be performed virtually any-where in the world (Giddens, 2000).

Thus, within half a century the concept of global knowledge economy has become firmly established. So has the desirability of this new economic model, which purports to replace capital with knowledge as the driver of economic growth (Brown and Lauder, 2006; Robertson 2005). This notion of knowledge-based, egalitarian meritocracy borders on a form of utopianism at times – as Brown and Lauder note,

> The rise of the global knowledge-based economy is believed to remove much of the source of conflict and strife between nations. Trade liberalization is presented as a 'win–win' opportunity for both developing and developed nations. (Brown and Lauder, 2006:26)

Thus, the concept of the knowledge economy also changed the way in which international development was conceptualized and planned. While modernization theory (Rostow, 1960) was predicated on the gradual development of industrial production techniques, integration into the global knowledge economy ostensibly offered the opportunity for rapid economic growth without the depletion of natural resources or development of industrial infrastructure. According to Giddens (2000:70), this means that 'societies can move from an agrarian to a knowledge style economy without passing through a phase of old style industrialization', a model sometimes known as 'leapfrog development' (Geng and Doberstein, 2008).

India's software industry offers one example of this phenomenon: by investing in the Indian Institutes of Technology (IITs), highly elite technical universities, in the 1950s and 1960s, the Indian government enabled the country to successfully compete with much higher-income countries in the global software industry some decades later. IITs created a set of highly skilled engineers with a globally competitive set of skills, leading to the establishment of a number of small software companies in the 1980s (Heeks, 1996). The development of internet communication catalysed this growth by allowing these companies to compete in global markets and find clients in relatively affluent countries such as the United States. Today, India's software industry contributes roughly 5 per cent of the country's GDP and employs some 4 million professionals in relatively well-paid jobs (Upadhya, 2009). The growth of India's software industry epitomizes the global nature of the knowledge economy, as well as the vital importance of education within.

Education in the global knowledge economy

As countries compete with one another in the global knowledge economy, their economic success is increasingly perceived as a result of their national education system and its ability to create globally competitive knowledge workers. As a result, there is a new emphasis on education as an agent of economic growth in both international organizations and national governments (Robertson, 2005). This has effectively created a discourse – a set of shared meanings, assumptions and taken-for-grated truths – around the concepts of education and the global knowledge economy (Fairclough, 1995). This discourse operates both on the global level through international organizations as well as on the national level through governments' educational policies and practices.

International organizations

As the concept of the global knowledge economy has gained currency, international organizations have reconceptualized and rearticulated their work in the education sector. All share a consensus that the advent of the knowledge economy creates new demands for education, particularly in the areas of lifelong learning and higher education (World Bank, 2003a; UNESCO 2005a). However, they differ in how they believe these demands should be addressed, and in some cases in their fundamental understanding of the knowledge economy itself.

Reflecting a perceived link between the knowledge economy and development, the World Bank has created its 'Knowledge for Development' programme that aims to support economic and social development by strengthening countries' ability to use knowledge to improve their economic competitiveness (World Bank Institute, 2008). According to the Bank, there are 'four pillars' that will allow countries to be successful in this respect:

1. Economic and Institutional Regime: Fair industry laws and regulations and a clear system of taxation and free-trade.
2. Educated and Skilled Population: Particularly to those completing secondary and tertiary education.
3. Information Infrastructure: Access to modern information technology and the internet.
4. Innovation System: Patents, scientific publications, and a system for ensuring royalty payments. (World Bank Institute, 2008)

To guide its funding in this area, the World Bank has developed a Knowledge Assessment Methodology (KAM), a set of quantitative procedures that produces the Knowledge Economy Index (KEI), a measure of a country's overall preparedness for the knowledge economy (World Bank Institute, 2008). According to the KEI, the top knowledge economies are mainly in Northern Europe (Denmark, Sweden, Finland, the Netherlands and Norway respectively occupy the top five places). The top-ranked country in Asia is 'Taiwan, China' (18th), followed closely by Singapore and Japan (19th and 20th, respectively). The bottom five countries are all in sub-Saharan Africa, respectively (World Bank, 2009).

To be successful in the global knowledge economy, the World Bank advocates lifelong learning, individualized instruction, digital technologies, and the importance of 'learning to learn' (World Bank, 2003a; Robertson, 2005). It also stresses the importance of higher education, which it claims 'helps countries build globally competitive economies by developing a skilled, productive and flexible labour force and by creating, applying, and spreading new ideas and technologies' (Salmi, 2009:2). Robertson (2005) points out that while these ideas emphasize individualism and choice, they contain a hidden agenda that seeks to replace institutional forms of education (e.g. schools and professional teachers) with market-based alternatives. With individualized learning through digital technologies, schools and teachers are no longer the 'gatekeepers of knowledge' but rather are artefacts of traditional, outdated modes of instruction that should be replaced (Robertson, 2005:162). Publicly funded education is associated with 'poor quality' and a 'fiscal burden' (although no evidence is provided to support this) while private alternatives are described as 'thriving' and associated with innovation (World Bank, 2003a:xviii). Robertson (2005) contrasts this with the view of the Organization for Economic Co-operation and Development (OECD), which also calls for individualized learning but is less critical of public institutions.

Other international organizations have been no less active in engaging with the knowledge economy discourse, although they differ in their particular recommendations. For example, UNESCO's (2005b) report *Towards Knowledge Societies* shares the World Bank's view that lifelong learning and higher education are essential to successful 'knowledge societies'. However, it also differs in several important respects: for example, UNESCO (2005a) employs the term 'knowledge *societies*' (as opposed to 'knowledge *economy*') to emphasize the social dimensions of the knowledge economy. The report also speaks of social inclusion, democratic participation, human rights, and development more than it refers to economic competitiveness, noting that knowledge is not only 'a tool for the satisfaction of economic needs' but also 'a constitutive component of development' (UNESCO, 2005a:27–8). While UNESCO shares the World Bank's emphasis on lifelong learning, it uses the phrase 'lifelong *education for all*' (UNESCO, 2005a:20), which highlights aspects of individual fulfilment and social participation rather than economic competitiveness. In addition to discussing higher education and technology, the report also discusses the importance of basic early childhood education, and its overall approach is governed more by social concerns than by the market, even warning that 'the risks of 'commoditization' of education 'are very real' (UNESCO, 2005a:87).

The influence of the knowledge economy discourse is also apparent at the regional level. For example, in 2000 the European Union created the Lisbon Strategy as a response to the perceived demands of the global knowledge economy. It aimed to make the European Union the 'most dynamic and competitive knowledge-based economy in the world' by 2010, in part by delivering a programme of lifelong learning emphasizing entrepreneurship, information technology, foreign languages and 'technological culture' (European Council, 2000). However, implementation of these lofty goals proved problematic – member states were unable to achieve targets set out in the strategy, leading to a major overhaul in 2005 (Borrás, 2009); by 2010 the strategy was widely regarded as a failure (Tausch, 2010)

National initiatives

As the knowledge economy discourse links economic growth to educational performance, improving national systems of education has become a key priority for governments throughout the world. Because of the global reach of the knowledge economy, this imperative applies to high- and low-income countries alike (World Bank, 2003a).

Mexico encompasses both of these extremes: rapid growth in manufacturing has created considerable wealth, yet income inequality is high and educational opportunities are unevenly distributed (Álvarez-Mendiola, 2006). In an effort to address the competitive pressures of the global knowledge economy, particularly those associated with the North American Free Trade Agreement, the government has focused on developing economic competitiveness through lifelong education. In 2000, it launched a programme titled Model of Education for Life and Work, which created centres that provide training in information technology and other vocational skills to adults. In 2002, this was followed by the establishment of National Council for Life and Work, which broadly focuses on coordinating the efforts of the country's many lifelong learning providers. However, Álvarez-Mendiola (2006:391) is critical of these initiatives, calling them 'half-hearted and uncoordinated' as well as lacking authority and resources. A 2008 World Bank report also seems unconvinced of their success, warning that

> if Mexico fails to devise an educational model that allows for lifelong learning through formal, informal, and non-formal formats, many workers may find themselves with obsolete training given the country's present pace of integration with the global knowledge economy. (Kuznetsov and Dahlman, 2008:62)

Even governments at the core of the global economy have worried about how to maintain international competitiveness in their education systems. For example, in 2009, US president Barack Obama launched the 'Educate to Innovate' initiative (Whitehouse, 2009), an effort to improve American students' performance in international achievement tests (see below) and prepare them for careers in science, technology, engineering and mathematics (STEM) related fields. The initiative relies on private sector partnerships to deliver a number of activities, such as educational television programming, a competition for educational video games, and a 'National Lab Day' to support 'hands-on inquiry-based lab experiences for students' (Whitehouse, 2009; National Science Teachers Association, 2010). As with Mexico, these initiatives are piecemeal and limited in scope, involving a series of relatively small-scale, special projects and programmes rather than substantial reform of mainstream education. As such, they are unlikely to create the desired improvement in achievement test scores across the country. Rather, the 'Education to Innovate' programme serves as a form of political rhetoric, associating the Obama administration with progress and economic growth without engaging in the controversial politics of genuine education reform.

While the ways in which both national governments and international organizations approach the knowledge economy differs in some respects, they share a common understanding of the global knowledge economy and the new economic role it ascribes to education. Furthermore, their educational prescriptions converge on a common set of themes: lifelong learning, higher education, individualism and choice. Finally, they are all looking for ways of measuring and comparing the educational achievements of countries, often through the use of international achievement tests.

International achievement tests

The important role of education in the global knowledge economy has created a new emphasis on measuring educational achievement and particularly on comparing and ranking educational achievement levels in different countries. This is not entirely a new phenomenon; in fact the history of international achievement tests dates back more than 50 years, roughly coinciding with early work on the knowledge economy by Drucker (1968) and Bell (1974). More recently, two international achievement tests, the Trends in International Mathematics and Science Studies (TIMSS) and the Programme for International Student Assessment (PISA) have received a great deal of attention from educators, policymakers and academics due to the large-scale, internationally comparable data that they produce.

Trends in International Mathematics and Science Study

The Trends in International Mathematics and Science Study (TIMSS) builds upon several decades of international achievement tests administered by the International Association for the Evaluation of Educational Achievement (abbreviated as IEA), an international research collaboration started in 1958 with support from the UNESCO Institute for Education (Wagemaker, 2004). In 1960, IEA conducted its first international achievement test, which covered four academic subjects (reading comprehension, mathematics, science and geography) and was administered to 9,918 students in 12 countries (Forshay et al., 1962).

Since then, IEA has continued to conduct numerous international achievement tests in subjects ranging from reading comprehension to computer literacy to science (Wagemaker, 2004). In 1995, it conducted its Third International Mathematics and Science Study, which has been repeated every four years since then under the name Trends in Mathematics and Science Study (TIMSS). TIMSS is administered to students in their fifth and ninth year of study (based on the US fourth and eighth grades); the number of countries participating in the study has increased from 45 in 1995 to 64 in 2011 (Mullis et al., 2009a). The 1995 and 2008 TIMSS also included an 'advanced' version that was administered to students in their second to last year of study, although only in a limited number of countries (Mullis et al., 2009a).

The focus of TIMSS is on curriculum mastery, and specifically on links between the 'intended curriculum' (as set forth by the government), the 'implemented curriculum' (through teachers and schools) and the 'attained curriculum' (as learned by students – Mullis et al., 2009b). For this reason, it not only measures students' learning but also collects data on teachers, school environments, curricula and students themselves; the 1999 TIMSS also included a video study of teaching styles in different countries (Stigler et al., 2000). This emphasis on curriculum mastery also means that the focus of the test is on students' understanding of the knowledge in a given subject area rather than the practical application or economic value of this knowledge.

Programme for International Student Assessment

In contrast to TIMSS, PISA specifically measures students' ability to apply knowledge in practical contexts that relate to 'everyday life' situations (OECD, 2000:9). The first test was carried out in 2000 and since then it has been repeated at three year intervals (OECD, 2009). PISA is run by the OECD, an international organization whose membership is composed of high-income, economically competitive countries. According to the OECD (2009) its main purpose is to provide internationally comparable data on student achievement, ideally contributing to a dialogue on effective policies for education.

PISA is administered to 15-year-olds in all participating countries, measuring their abilities in three different areas: scientific literacy, mathematical literacy and reading literacy (OECD, 2000). The term 'literacy' is used for each subject area to denote a practical emphasis. PISA claims to measure students' 'preparedness for adult life' and to 'focus on the knowledge, understanding and skills required for effective functioning in everyday life' (OECD, 2000:9). This focus is closely related to the view of education as an agent of economic growth in the knowledge economy. Since the first test in 2000, the programme has been repeated every three years, increasing from 43 'countries/economies'[1] in 2000 to 65 in 2009 (OECD, 2009).

International achievement tests and policy debates

The results of international achievement tests have given policymakers a new means of comparing their education system to those of other countries and borrowing policies that appear to work well elsewhere. Grek terms this the

'PISA effect' referring to the 'ways in which PISA enters . . . national policy spaces and acts on them in ways that govern and shape education activity' (Grek, 2009:24). Often, poor PISA results or a slip in global rankings, evidence that the education system is failing and that reform is needed, are used as a call to action.

For example, in 2010 the Secretary of State for Education in England and Wales, Michael Gove (2010), wrote a letter in the *Times Educational Supplement* calling the United Kingdom's falling place in the 2009 PISA rankings a 'spur to action'. According to Gove (2010), PISA also 'provides clear pointers to how we can reform our schools' system to make it one of the best in the world'; these pointers include decentralization, competition between schools, and accountability through standardized testing. All of these strategies featured prominently in the White Paper recently released by the Department for Education; thus PISA ostensibly supports and vindicates Gove's policies. His analysis carefully omits alternative interpretations: for example, Gove cites Finland as a model country, its consistently high performance in PISA has prompted many to look to the Finnish education system as a model for reform (Anderson, 2011). However, contrary to Gove's recommendations, Finland has no national testing programme or competitive school league tables, and education is centrally regulated rather than decentralized (West and Ylönen, 2010). Gove (2010) selectively omits these key differences when arguing for more decentralization and standardized testing as 'clear pointers' to making England's education system 'one of the best in the world'.

Gove's comments on PISA show how international achievement tests can be used to legitimate reforms that are undertaken for ideological reasons, rather than serving as a source for genuine policy dialogue as the OECD envisages (OECD, 2000). As Grek (2009:34) notes, results are 'used to justify, change or provide support for existing policy direction' rather than engage in genuine comparative study. While the tests themselves are not responsible for this, their claim to objectivity, which Grek (2009:25) calls a 'taken-for grant-edness' inherently lends them to such misinterpretation. The very notion of an international achievement test is predicated on a universal notion of achievement: the idea that to do well in education means the same thing in every social context, and, by extension, that education fulfils the same role in every society. Through its use of language, PISA implies that the universal purpose of education is economic rather than social or individual fulfilment: 'economies' not 'societies' participate in the test, and essential 'preparedness for adult life' is construed largely in terms of solving problems of scientific reasoning and finance (OECD, 2000:9). Thus, the tests are constructed in a way that equates educational success with economic growth, an idea that is susceptible to criticism.

Reflective Exercise

- Do you think international achievement tests are useful? If so, for whom (teachers, parents, economists, curriculum writers, policymakers, etc.), and why?

Critical perspectives on the knowledge economy

Today, the emergence and existence of a global knowledge economy has achieved the status of uncontested fact: while policymakers may differ on how they seek to address the competitive pressures it brings, few doubt the need to do so. However, as Robertson notes, there is a tendency to reify the knowledge economy as if it were 'not only an unproblematic idea but an unproblematic reality' (Robertson, 2005:166). In fact, the concept of the knowledge economy and the assumptions that underpin it are deeply problematic, far more so than the relatively simple policy responses generally acknowledge.

As it is constructed in official documents (e.g. World Bank, 2003a) the global knowledge economy is far from value-neutral. On the contrary, it embeds a strong neoliberal view of globalization (Friedman, 2006): the belief that the spread of global capitalism is both inevitable and egalitarian, that competition creates better lives for everyone, and that economic growth is always desirable. It also has epistemological ramifications: global knowledge economy discourses privilege certain types of knowledge and ways of knowing. Economically productive knowledge, particularly relating to science and technology, is valued; other types of knowledge, for example critical thinking and democratic citizenship are implicitly unvalued by the relatively little attention they receive in official documents. As the examples of World Bank documents and Gove's comments on PISA show, the knowledge economy is often cited to legitimate reforms that promote free-market competition and decrease the role of state institutions in educational provision.

Reflecting the problematic nature of the global knowledge economy itself, attempts to improve economic competiveness through investment in education (whether by governments or individuals) do not necessarily lead to improved employment and economic growth. Rather, a greater supply of qualified labour increases competition for a limited supply of jobs, creating a 'race to the bottom' in terms of wages and working conditions. Brown and Lauder (2006:41) describe this as a 'paradox of human capital' in which an increase in the global supply of well-qualified knowledge workers leads to a decrease in their value in the labour market, resulting in downward pressures on salaries and diminishing returns on educational investments. Brown et al. (2011) compare this process to a 'Dutch auction' (one in which the price is continually lowered until a bidder will accept), whereby countries and individuals must continually drive down salaries in order attract global employers and maintain employment. However, the emphasis on individualism combined with a diminished role of the state in economic coordination results in individuals bearing the brunt of this downward spiral:

> The focus on individual employability (supply side) rather than a political commitment to job creation (demand side) is a political sleight of hand that shifts the responsibility for employment firmly onto the shoulders of individuals rather than the state. (Brown and Lauder, 2006:46)

Thus, increased participation in higher education is not reflective of new economic prospects for graduates, but rather indicative of individuals trying to outcompete one another to obtain desirable jobs.

Knowledge economy discourses have not only changed education but also led to a fundamental redefinition of knowledge itself. Rather than a public good, knowledge becomes a private commodity, 'intellectual property', which can be bought and sold much like any other item. This redefinition is questionable, as Simon Marginson (2010:32) points out, knowledge is a 'non-rivalrous' commodity: it can be used by any number of people without being depleted in the way that a tangible commodity (i.e. food, oil, clothing) would be. While the concept of knowledge as private property is presented as a moral issue, it is deeply problematic in practice. For example, for several years the application of WTO's TRIPS to antiretroviral drugs used to treat HIV threatened to make these medicines unaffordable for residents of low-income countries, and have likely inflated the prices of generic alternatives (Love, 2007). The real motivation is more profit than morality, as it is only through this redefinition that knowledge becomes something profitable, something through which those in positions of power can seek to extend and increase their influence. Reflecting this viewpoint, Jessop (2002:13–4) calls knowledge a 'fictitious commodity' that is 'artificially made scarce' through a set of intellectual property laws that restrict its mobility and application.

Summary

Over the past half-century, a number of scholars (Machlup, 1962; Drucker, 1968) have described the advent of a global knowledge economy, an increase in economic activity that focuses on the production and application of knowledge, information and intellectual property. This idea has become widely accepted among international organizations, national governments and other educational policymakers, who see education as a key factor in creating a population of knowledge workers who can compete in this new economic landscape. Education is increasingly considered in relation to national economic competitiveness, particularly in the areas of lifelong learning and higher education (World Bank, 2003a; Salmi, 2009).

The global knowledge economy has also resulted in increased interest in international achievement tests such as the Trends in Mathematics and Science Study (TIMSS) and PISA. These are administered to students in many countries around the world, producing a body of internationally comparable data that ostensibly allows the ranking of national education systems. Policymakers draw upon this data when discussing educational reforms, although this is often used to legitimate existing policy decisions that are driven primarily by political ideology.

While the global knowledge economy has become a key driver of educational policymaking at all levels, its deeply problematic nature is seldom acknowledged. The global knowledge economy is not a value-neutral concept; it embeds contentious notions of global capitalism and neoliberalism under the pretence of progressive social change that is desirable and inevitable. Many of these characteristics are seen in changing discourses on Information and Communication Technology (ICT) in education, which are explored in the next chapter.

Reflective Exercise

Reflect on the following set of questions relating to education and the global knowledge economy:

1. Do you believe that a country's economic success and the well-being of its residents are tied to how well its education system performs in relation to other countries?
2. Is education a human right, a public service or a personal investment? Which of these views most closely fits the 'knowledge economy' discourse and why?
3. Should information be treated like other types of property (e.g. clothing, cars)? What are the implications of this for students, educators, the private sector and the general public?

Useful websites

www.iea.nl – The IEA, which runs TIMSS. Last accessed on 4 May 2012.

www.pisa.oecd.org – The OECD's website on PISA. Last accessed on 4 May 2012.

Note

1 PISA uses the term countries/economies to describe participants, as in same cases they are territories within a country (e.g. Tamil Nadu in India and Shanghai in China). In contrast, TIMSS uses the term 'education system' to describe its participants, which are generally nation-states.

7 International Discourses on ICT in Education

Chapter Outline

Introduction

In 1999, Sugata Mitra, an accomplished Indian computer scientist, tried a bold experiment that few others would have had the ingenuity or temerity to undertake. He placed a computer inside a small hole in a wall in a New Delhi slum. As the slums are famous for their poverty and lawlessness, many would simply have expected the experiment to end in the lamented loss of a valuable computer. However, what Mitra found was that children in the slum taught themselves to use the computer with no adult supervision. Furthermore, without any formal instruction they used the computer for a range of educational purposes (Mitra, 2003).

The 'hole in the wall' experiment illustrates a larger trend in the relationship between technology and education: new Information and Communication

Technologies (ICTs) are increasingly viewed as a catalyst in socio-economic development. This chapter discusses and analyses the use of ICT for education and development. It begins by looking at the origins of technology in education, then looks at the emergence of a discourse that looks to ICT as a means to achieve poverty reduction, social inclusion and other forms of socio-economic development. After looking at some leading programmes and initiatives in this area, the chapter presents critical responses to ICT in education and questions whether many of the promises about its potential will, in fact, ever materialize.

Technology and education

Using technology to improve education has been a subject of interest for many years. As computer technology developed throughout the latter half of the twentieth century, innovative educators sought ways to exploit its potential. Among the first to do so was Seymour Papert, a mathematician at the Massachusetts Institute of Technology (MIT), who developed some of the first educational computer programs in the early 1970s. Papert's work built upon constructivist models of learning, which he expanded in his own theory of constructionism. In essence, constructionism claims that learners are able to learn best by creating interactive models of the world around them. Rather than mastering a set curriculum, Papert asserts that 'the kind of knowledge children most need is the kind of knowledge that will help them to get more knowledge' (Papert, 1993:139). To Papert, ICT represents one of the most effective environments for enabling this kind of interactive, self-directed learning. Papert's work marked the beginning of an increased interest in education and ICTs, particularly computers and the internet (Edwards, 2012).

Internationally, many countries have rushed to integrate ICT into their education system in order to ensure an internationally competitive workforce. In a study of the international spread of ICT education policies, Ham and Cha (2009) report that by the year 2000, 68.7 per cent of countries had established a policy on ICT education, compared to just 11.9 per cent in 1981. Ironically, whether or not ICT is effective in improving education may have little to do with its rapid spread: what is more important is the extent to which it is *perceived* to be important to education in economically successful countries. As

Ham and Cha (2009:551) note in their study, 'Nation-states tend to model themselves after other countries that are perceived to be successful or legitimate as "reference societies"', which can lead to the adoption of ICT in education as a form of policy mimicry.

In contrast to the rapid spread of ICT in national education systems, many researchers (e.g. James, 2003; Pratt-Adams et al., 2010; Edwards, 2012) have spoken of a global 'digital divide' in reference to the large inequalities in access to ICT between the world's rich and poor. For instance, according to the World Bank (2012c) less than 2 per cent of people in Afghanistan have access to the internet, while in Sweden this number is 88 per cent. In theory, the digital divide also creates the risk of a continual vicious cycle: those with access to ICT will develop economically valuable skills and eventually go on to secure higher-paying jobs, while the world's poor will lack these opportunities and become even more 'left behind'.

The social benefits of technology have been a source of interest since the idea of international development first took hold in the mid-twentieth century (see Chapter 1). Stambach and Malekela (2006:324) note that in early international development programmes the UN and United States 'stressed the need to use western technology to foster cultural change in what economists of the time routinely referred to as "backward areas"'. Reflecting this worldview, Schramm (1964) looked at how access to mass media and communication technology relates to development. By establishing correlations between communications technology and mass media with economic growth, he suggested that spreading access to such technology would contribute to development.

 International development organizations have looked to technology to expand access to education: UNESCO (Tacchi and Slater, 2004), USAID (2004) and DFID (2001) have all run programmes that use the radio to deliver distance education to areas that lack schools, or where students do not attend due to household commitments. However, largely due to its high costs, the use of new ICTs (e.g. computers and the internet) received little consideration in these programmes. From the donors' standpoint, these programmes represented poor value for money as the high cost of new technologies was at odds with the goal of expanding enrolment (Shields 2011); concentrated investment in technology would improve quality for a few, but reduce the ability of many to access education.

The digital divide and ICT for development

By the close of the twentieth century, the availability of new ICTs (i.e. computers, mobile phones and the internet) had increased throughout much of the world. Facilitated in part by competition between manufacturers and global free trade, the availability of computer hardware increased in many countries while its price fell considerably. At the same time, new wireless technologies began to rapidly spread connectivity throughout many low-income countries. Because they require less investment in physical infrastructure, these technologies were particularly successful in connecting large numbers of people in low-income countries. Data from the International Telecommunications Union (ITU) show that the number of mobile phone users in Africa increased by over 400 per cent between 2005 and 2011, while the expansion of land lines was significantly lower at 20 per cent (ITU, 2012).

This rapid expansion of ICT into developing countries prompted a surge of interest in the potential of new technologies to facilitate social and economic development, leading to increased calls to 'bridge the global digital divide' (James, 2003). Reflecting a broader reconceptualization of development as poverty reduction and social inclusion (Sen, 1999, see Chapter 2), many (e.g. James, 2003; DFID 2001; Tacchi and Slater, 2004) began to assert that expanding access to ICTs in low-income countries would reduce poverty, improve education, facilitate social participation and democracy and lead to the creation of an inclusive global information society. This viewpoint was evident in initiatives by major international donors (DFID, 2001; USAID, 2004) focusing on the use of 'ICT for development' (ICT4D as the movement has been called in the development sector, World Bank, 2003b).

A major milestone in the emergence of 'ICT4D' was the World Summit on Information Society (WSIS), two high-level conferences endorsed by the UN General Assembly that sought to establish the foundations for an inclusive, global information society made possible through expanded access to ICT. Involving many world leaders and prominent figures from the international development sector, the WSIS was held in two phases: the first in Geneva in 2003 and a follow-up in Tunisia in 2005. Each phase produced a key document: the Geneva Declaration of Principles put forward a consensus vision of what an equitable global information society would look like and how it would function, while the Tunis Commitment offered a concrete pledge to attain this vision (World Summit on Information Society, 2003, 2005).

The language of these documents is illustrative of a new approach to ICT and development in which the emphasis is on social equity, inclusion and poverty reduction. The WSIS documents repeatedly emphasize the need to include marginalized groups and reduce the number of people living in poverty, claiming that technology offers economic benefits not only to the world's rich but also to its poor. In terms of education, this has meant shifting attention from high achievement (the traditional focus of ICT in education) to expanded access.

For instance, the Tunis Commitment makes the claim that:

> ICTs have enormous potential to expand access to quality education, to boost literacy and universal primary education, and to facilitate the learning process itself, thus laying the groundwork for the establishment of a fully inclusive and development-oriented Information Society and knowledge economy which respects cultural and linguistic diversity. (World Summit on Information Society, 2005:2)

These claims create a utopian vision of education and development: ICT is used to expand and improve education, which in turn supports social cohesion through the global information society and economic growth through the knowledge economy. Even the status of linguistic and cultural minorities is protected, but are all these claims realistic? This is a statement of a perceived potential about what ICTs *can* do, it is stated as fact, but in reality these outcomes are highly debatable. This divide between rhetoric and reality is further discussed in the section on critical approaches to ICT in education below.

The case for ICT in international education

Proponents of ICT for education in developing countries (e.g. James, 2003; DFID, 2001; Tacchi and Slater, 2004; USAID, 2004) put forward several compelling arguments to their position, which are presented below. These arguments support the view that using ICT for education is an entirely positive proposition: there are many benefits to its use and no real downsides. In the discourse on the subject, the rationales for using ICTs are blended and interlinked such than the combined benefits of ICT are greater than the sum of its impact in individual areas. This section examines the argument for ICT from three different perspectives: expanding access to education, improving educational quality and promoting international dialogue and global citizenship.

Access

Continued challenges in achieving Education For All (EFA – UNESCO, 2011) suggest that conventional approaches (i.e. schools, teachers and textbooks) may not be sufficient. On the other hand, ICT may offer alternatives that are more realistic, efficient and effective. For instance, electronic textbooks stored on computers could offer an appealing alternative to traditional paper books: in addition to possible educational advantages of the interactive multimedia activities that are possible on a computer, the money saved on buying textbooks could actually offset the cost of the computer purchase.

Similarly, ICT has the potential to address the shortage of qualified teachers, a problem in many rural areas: interactive, project-based activities on computers can allow for student-led, self-directed learning. In schools that lack qualified teachers in particular subjects (e.g. secondary level science or mathematics), untrained teachers can assume the role of facilitators, guiding students through an ICT-based project or activity without having subject-specific expertise themselves. Another alternative is teleteaching, using low-cost webcams and the internet, students in schools that lack qualified teachers can virtually 'sit in' on classes in other schools (DFID, 2001; USAID, 2004).

Quality

With expanded global free trade and the growth of knowledge industries, ICT is increasingly seen as necessary to educate a workforce that is competitive in the global economy (see Chapter 6). In high- and low-income countries alike, the skilled use of ICT is seen as attracting high-paying jobs that attract employers and spur economic growth (Brown and Lauder, 2006). From this perspective, the benefits of ICT are two-fold, as it is both curriculum content and a medium of instruction.

The study of ICT as a curriculum subject was initially associated with efforts to improve computer literacy (Cuban, 2001; Goodson and Mangan, 1996:65). However, Cuban (2001:177) notes that 'no consensus . . . exists on exactly what computer literacy is' and that 'among computer advocates, definitions diverge considerably'. While drawing an implicit analogy to other forms of literacy (i.e. language), notions of computer literacy fail to indicate what type of technology (including hardware and software) a 'literate' student should be able to use and – more importantly – what they should be able to do with this technology (Goodson and Mangan, 1996). As an alternative to the relatively simplistic notion of literacy, Prensky (2001) defines the concept of a 'digital native' in reference to those born when modern ICTs were already widespread. Unlike 'digital immigrants' (members of older generations), learning to use technology is essentially second nature to digital natives, and they require little formal training to order to use new technology effectively.

As a medium of instruction, ICT improves the quality of learning in other subject areas by allowing students to construct models, experiment with these models, interact with others and collaborate. This perspective on ICT and education underpinned Papert's early research (1980), which involved teaching children computer programming as a way to construct mental models and facilitate problem solving. Perhaps more importantly, ICT facilitates 'learning to learn' (Ackerman, 2001:1): as students use computers to construct models and solve problems, they are able to reflect upon and improve the ways that they learn.

Inclusion

New ICTs have made it easier and less expensive to communicate with others around the world, creating new educational opportunities. Virtually any two classrooms with a computer and internet connection instantaneously communicate with one another via videoconferencing (e.g. Skype), allowing students to participate in discussions or to work collaboratively with their peers around the world. Such interaction is of particular interest in the area of global citizenship education, which concerns issues of individuals' rights, responsibilities, choices and actions from a global perspective. Global citizenship education often involves the discussion of international human rights issues and asking students how their actions affect those in other countries.

Naturally, the ability to instantly communicate with students on the other side of the world opens up new possibilities for global citizenship education: discussions of global issues are more relevant when they include students in other countries, who may bring new perspectives or be affected by global issues in different ways. From this perspective, ICT is not just educationally beneficial but also a moral imperative: to exclude students from access to ICT and the internet denies them a voice in discussions of global citizenship and the larger global information society.

Reflective Exercise

- Do you think ICT can be used to expand access to education and improve educational quality? Can ICT contribute to poverty alleviation? If so, how?

Case study: One Laptop Per Child

Perhaps nothing has generated more interest in ICT for education in the international development sector than the One Laptop Per Child (OLPC) Association, whose mission is 'to empower the children of developing countries to learn by providing one connected laptop to every school-age child' (OLPC, 2011). Started by Nicholas Negroponte, a professor at the MIT's media labs, OLPC has developed a low-cost laptop called the XO that it believes can theoretically revolutionize education in low-income countries. When first introduced, the idea of a '$100 laptop' for the world's poorest children captivated much attention from the media, international development community and public alike. With very low power consumption, and a screen that works well in direct sunlight, the design of the laptop is aimed at the difficult contexts common in many low-income countries. Additionally, all software installed on the laptop is open source, meaning it is not subject to expensive royalties or licensing fees, and any software developer who chooses to do so can modify and redistribute its code.

The OLPC Project is heavily influenced by Papert's (1980) theory of constructionism, and for this reason programming languages designed for children are integral to the XO's software. Speaking in 2007, Negroponte asserted, 'Kids don't program enough and . . . if there's anything I hope this brings back it's programming to kids, it's really important . . . programming is absolutely fundamental' (Negroponte, 2007). Collaboration and connectivity are also key elements of its approach: the XO laptop is equipped with mesh networking technology, which allows an XO user to communicate with other users in the vicinity. This allows sharing of information and collaboration even in areas that lack an internet connection.

While it appears that every consideration has been taken into account (even the laptop itself is made of materials that pose minimal environmental threat), OLPC has had difficulty reaching many of its targets. First promoted as a '$100 laptop for the world's poor', it has in reality never come close to its $100 target. In 2007 Negroponte claimed, 'It will be $100. In two years. it will go below $100' (Negroponte, 2007), yet more than two years later the price still exceeded $200 (Bray, 2009). Furthermore, the laptop price did not include related costs such as internet access and power, which can be particularly expensive in low-income countries (Shields, 2009).

Finding buyers of the XO also proved more difficult than first anticipated; plans to launch the XO in six countries were delayed after the respective governments failed to place orders. Instead, OLPC has launched the XO in smaller numbers in Uruguay, Peru, Rwanda and Argentina. Uruguay was the first country to launch the XO in practice, ordering 100,000 laptops in 2007 and 200,000 more in 2009. The laptop is used as part of its Plan CEIBAL, which aims to expand ICT and online learning in primary schools. While Negroponte (2007) set a goal to manufacture 1 million XO laptops per month by 2008, actual production has remained at a fraction of initial expectations (Talbot, 2008).

The idea of a low-cost laptop quickly gained attention and sparked a number of similar initiatives. The microprocessor manufacturer Intel, once a partner in OLPC, has developed its Classmate line of low-cost laptops targeted at educational use. More recently, the Indian Ministry of Human Resource Development announced plans for its Aakash Tablet (*aakash* is a Hindi word that means 'sky'), a small touch screen computer that it claims can be provided to children for as little as $35 (BBC, 2010). Following a limited pilot production in 2011 of approximately 1,000 units, the programme plans to produce an updated version in 2012 (Anwer, 2012).

Critical perspectives on ICT and education

The potential of ICT to improve education in low-income countries is inspiring and appears to hold much potential, yet is it really as good as it seems? More than eight years have passed since the WSIS (2003) in Geneva, and many more since Papert's (1980) early work with computers and education, yet it seems that education is continually on the verge of a technological revolution that never quite materializes. In light of this divide between rhetoric and reality, it is worth taking a critical look at whether the promise of ICT is all that seems.

On one hand, it remains dubious whether the claims of advocates of ICT about its potential to improve education are supported by evidence. So much of what has been said revolves around what ICTs supposedly *can do*, not on evidence of what they actually *do*. In practice, benefits of ICT in education are difficult to identify and measure, raising the question of whether they actually exist at all. A study funded by the World Bank's Information for Development Program identified this mismatch between theoretical beliefs about ICT's potential and observed outcomes, stating 'Research on impacts of ICTs on student achievement yields few conclusive statements, pro or contra, about the use of ICTs in education' (Trucano, 2005:7).

Even in high-income countries, where educational research is more prevalent and better funded, studies on ICT have yielded few conclusive documents. In his study of ICT in California schools, Larry Cuban, a professor at Stanford University, found that 'no clear and substantial evidence of students increasing their academic achievement as a result of using information technologies' (Cuban, 2001:133). In fact, in many cases ICT was relatively peripheral to learning, as teachers 'adapted an innovation to fit their customary practices' (Cuban, 2001:97), rather than fundamentally changing their approach to teaching. Cuban's findings raise the question of whether it is appropriate or ethical to invest resources in educational technology, particularly in low-income countries where funding for education is already scarce. The idea of low-cost computing laptops appeals to consumer enthusiasm for cheap technology that is prevalent in high-income countries, but the economics seem less appealing when the realities of educational funding in low-income countries are taken into account. For instance, annual expenditure per primary school student in Bangladesh and Ethiopia is less than $50 per year, meaning that purchasing a $100 laptop for each child would consume 2 years' entire budget for those students, leaving no funding for teachers or schools. This does not even take into account additional costs that would be incurred, such as power and internet connection fees. In light of this economics, the conclusion of Cuban's study, that 'the investment of billions of dollars over the last decade has yet to produce worthy outcomes' (Cuban, 2001:197), could serve as a poignant warning to international development donors (e.g. USAID, the World Bank and DFID).

On the other hand, there is good reason to question whether the discourse is in fact as high-minded and idealistic as it first seems. While documents such as the Tunis Commitment make bold claims about the ability of ICT to 'expand access to quality education, to boost literacy and universal primary education, and to facilitate the learning process itself' they also embed a set of unstated, implicit values that are of equal importance (World Summit on Information Society, 2005:2). For instance, initiatives to spread access to ICT are often linked to individual ownership of technology (i.e. One Laptop per Child), and could be interpreted as an expansion of technological consumerism. The 50x15 foundation, a programme initiated by microprocessor manufacturer AMD to bring ICT to education in low-income countries, explicitly states, 'bridging the digital divide isn't just an act of goodwill: it's good business' (50x15 Foundation, 2010). By supporting the spread of ICTs, multinational technology companies (e.g. Intel and AMD) are also building their future consumer base. Furthermore, by preparing students to compete in the global knowledge economy, these companies are also training their future workforce.

More broadly, the support for 'ICT4D' conflates consumer-driven enthusiasm for low-cost technology with the humanitarian aims of poverty reduction and social inclusion. Most work in the field assumes that complex social problems (e.g. poverty and illiteracy) can be remedied by providing access to ICT. In doing so, they ignore hierarchical social and geopolitical relationships that are at the root of these problems, and it is no surprise that Stambach and Malekela (2006:333) assert that 'the disjuncture between policy and reality is perhaps as great as what is perceived to be the distance spanning the "digital divide"'.

Reflective Exercise

- To date, the use of ICT has not produced the improvement in outcomes that many predicted, nor has it spread as quickly as they hoped. Why do you think this is the case?

Summary

This chapter has examined the use of ICT for education, with an emphasis on ICTs as part of development initiatives in low-income countries. Proponents of ICT4D have claimed that bridging the global digital divide will reduce poverty, improve education and spur economic growth, and the UN's WSIS made commitments to bridge this divide. Education has been a key focus of this discussion, with particular emphasis on the ability of ICT to expand access to education, improve the quality of education, and support social inclusion. Many of these beliefs are central to the work of the OLPC Association (OLPC, 2011), which aims to provide children in low-income countries with its XO Laptop. While the laptop features a rugged design appropriate for low-income countries and software built on the constructionist theories of Seymour Papert (1980), it has yet to receive the widespread take-up that OLPC originally anticipated.

However, there are legitimate grounds to question the use of ICT for education in international development. First, many of the claims about the educational benefits of ICT have never materialized: there are many statements about what ICT *can do* but little evidence of what it actually *does*. Furthermore, there are many implicit values embedded in the high-minded and idealistic discourse on ICT for development, which often proposes technological solutions to complex social issues that stem from deeply rooted inequalities.

Reflective Exercise

Review the passage from the WSIS Tunis Commitment quoted below. Do you agree or disagree with its arguments? If you agree, where is the evidence to support these claims? If you disagree, why do you think that the authors of the Tunis Commitment believed this?

ICTs have enormous potential to expand access to quality education, to boost literacy and universal primary education, and to facilitate the learning process itself, thus laying the groundwork for the establishment of a fully inclusive and development-oriented Information Society and knowledge economy which respects cultural and linguistic diversity (World Summit on Information Society, 2005).

Useful websites

http://bit.ly/TEDOLPC – A video of Nicholas Negroponte speaking about the OLPC project. Last accessed on 4 May 2012.

http://blogs.worldbank.org/edutech – The World Bank's blog on educational technology. Last accessed on 4 May 2012.

http://hole-in-the-wall.com – Sugata Mitra's 'hole in the wall' project. Last accessed on 4 May 2012.

http://laptop.org – The OLPC project. Last accessed on 4 May 2012.

8 Globalization and Higher Education

Introduction

The preceding chapters have shown how national governments and international organizations have come to see education as central to their economic success. Concepts such as the global knowledge economy have also had important ramifications in the higher education sector. Governments have looked to universities to act as catalysts for knowledge-intensive industries, both through teaching highly specialized skills and by creating economically valuable knowledge through their research. This challenges the role of universities as institutions that are primarily concerned with the pursuit of knowledge and truth for its own sake, redefining them as agents of economic growth. Additionally, there is a growing expectation that, in order to be successful, universities must become international institutions with teaching and research links that span the globe.

This chapter discusses a series of global trends in higher education. It begins by analysing how expanding access to higher education has coincided with a decline in public funding for universities, and then continues to discuss a new set of international dimensions in higher education. The implications of the World Trade Organization's (WTO's) controversial General Agreement on Trade in Services (GATS) are discussed in detail, and the chapter analyses new regional trends in international higher education before concluding.

Higher education in the global knowledge economy

The twentieth century witnessed a rapid expansion of higher education in most countries of the world. In 1900 there were just 500,000 university students enrolled in higher education worldwide, roughly one in every hundred young persons aged 18 to 23. One hundred years later that number had increased to 100 million – 20 per cent of the same age group (Schofer and Meyer, 2005). The growth in student enrolments was mirrored in a growth in institutions: of the 9,000 universities in existence today, approximately 59 per cent were founded post-1950 (Gürüz, 2008). This dramatic rise can be attributed to a number of factors, including an increase in jobs that required specialized technical skills, an expansion of primary and secondary schooling, and the spread of cultural values that prized personal knowledge and lifelong learning (Schofer and Meyer, 2005).

In many cases, this rapid expansion also fundamentally changed the nature of higher education. For centuries, universities had justified their existence as institutions for the pursuit of truth and acquisition of knowledge; the image of the 'ivory tower' had little to do with practical social and economic concerns. However, the growth of knowledge economy discourses (see Chapter 6) recast universities as producers of commodified knowledge that drives economic growth. For example, in 2007 the United Kingdom's policymaking on higher education was separated from the Department of Children, Schools and Families (DCSF), which was responsible for all other educational policies, and placed in the newly created Department for University, Skills and Innovation, renamed the Department for Business Innovation and Skills in 2009. The UK government's 2009 strategy paper, titled *Higher Ambition: The Future of Universities in a Knowledge Economy*, declared,

> We compete on knowledge – its creation, its acquisition, and its transformation
> into commercially successful uses. . . . In a knowledge economy, universities
> are the most important mechanism we have for generating and preserving,
> disseminating, and transforming knowledge into wider social and economic
> benefits. (Department for Business, Innovation and Skills, 2009:3, 7)

This demonstrates the dual importance of universities in the global knowledge economy. First, they provide graduates with skills that are valuable to employers, essentially producing specialized forms of human capital. Additionally, universities engage in research, creating knowledge that private businesses can utilize in commercialized products and services. In both cases, universities become economically rationalized institutions: their existence is justified by their supposed ability to make certain economic outcomes for individuals and governments (i.e. more desirable employment and increased economic productivity).

The economic rationalization of the university brought an associated set of changes in the way higher education was funded. Under the arrangements of the 'welfare state', governments considered higher education as a public good: enrolment was restricted to a relatively small number of individuals and was funded by the government in the belief that the benefits of this education would extend to the entire country (Portnoi et al., 2010). However, in the context of the global knowledge economy, the questions of who benefits from higher education and who is responsible to fund it are more complex. While national governments continue to enjoy rewards from a well-educated workforce through high levels of employment, individuals also benefit immensely from higher education by gaining access to more desirable, better paid employment. In low-income countries, the individual benefits of higher education are manifested in 'brain drain': the emigration of skilled professionals (many of whom received a state-funded higher education) to higher income countries in search of better employment opportunities (Altbach, 2004).

Private sector businesses – particularly those in fields related to science, technology, engineering and mathematics (STEM) – also benefit from a supply of highly skilled workers (Brown and Lauder, 2006). These benefits to the individual and private sector have supported an argument that higher education is more of a private commodity than a public good. Phillips and Schweissfurth (2008:70) summarize this case as follows:

> Overall, the higher the level of education, the greater the benefit to the
> individual . . . [higher] education, which brings the highest returns to the

individual, through the potential for securing high-paying employment, tends to be perceived as a sector less deserving of high levels of public expenditure, with greater cost-sharing by the ultimate beneficiary, the individual.

Conservative governments in the United States and United Kingdom used this rationale to justify a reduction in public funding from the 1980s onward, meaning that students increasingly paid for the cost of their education through tuition fees.

These combined contexts – the rapid expansion of higher education, its economic rationalization and a decline in state funding – have created a situation favourable to the internationalization of higher education. As state support for higher education has deteriorated, universities have looked beyond their national borders to secure funding, experimenting with new models of teaching, research and partnership. This expansion has resulted in a new set of international dimensions to higher education.

International dimensions to higher education

The internationalization of higher education is complex and difficult to fully chart, as the nature of internationalization varies between countries and institutions (Welch, 2002). However, four common trends are prevalent throughout much of the world: international student enrolment; global university rankings; methods of offshore delivery and global research networks.

International student mobility

Nothing better exemplifies the internationalization of higher education than the phenomenal growth of international students in higher education. Like higher education enrolment in general, the number of university students who go abroad has increased rapidly in recent years. In 1950 there were only 107,000 international students throughout the world; by 1999 this had increased tenfold to 1.4 million, and in 2008 the total exceeded 3 million (Barnett and Wu, 1995; UNESCO Institute for Statistics, 2011b). To provide some perspective, the number of students who go abroad for education is roughly equivalent to the population of a medium city, larger than St. Louis, Brussels, Kyoto or Vancouver (UNPD, 2009).

The global rise of international student mobility is intertwined with larger trends in globalization, the global knowledge economy, and the internationalization of higher education. Many of the larger changes associated with globalization, for instance increased international migration and the falling cost of international transport and communication, make international study more feasible than it would have been several decades ago (IOM, 2008). Similarly, the context of the global knowledge economy has created a premium for degrees from prestigious, 'world class' universities (Brown and Lauder, 2006). In making choices about higher education, students will tend to pursue options that they believe offer the greatest leverage in achieving their personal and career aspirations. As a recent report from the International Organization for Migration claims, students see international study as a 'boost to their career in both their home country and on the international job market' (IOM, 2008:105). Finally, decreased public funding for higher education and the commodified view of education supported by GATS, mean that universities throughout the world are actively seeking to recruit international students, matching supply with the demand.

By far, the majority of students travel to destinations in the 'Global North' – Western Europe, North America, Australia and New Zealand (IOM, 2008). English speaking countries have a particular advantage in attracting international students (Altbach, 2004): in 2003 five English Speaking countries (The United States, United Kingdom, Canada, Australia and New Zealand) received 47 per cent of all international students (Böhm et al., 2004). In contrast, many international students come from countries in Asia: China and India account for the largest number of outgoing students with totals of 432,559 and 180,456 (a combined 22.5% of all outgoing students) respectively. They are followed by South Korea, Germany, Japan and the United States as the major countries of origin for international students (UNESCO Institute for Statistics, 2011b).

However, some evidence suggests that the advantage of major destination countries may be weakening: while countries in the Global North receive the majority of international students, growth rates in other countries have been very high. Between 2002 and 2007 growth in international student enrolment in China, India, and South Korea (30.1%, 47.4% and 60.7%, respectively) far outpaced those in the United States and United Kingdom (0.8% and 9.2% respectively – Shields and Edwards, 2010). These new destinations offer a number of advantages to potential students: in many cases they are closer to students' home country, reducing travel expenses. Additionally, tuition fees and the cost of living may be significantly lower than more established destinations, while visa restrictions and the potential for post-work employment can be more favourable. Rapid growth of these new destinations is increasing competitive pressure to recruit international students, and over time may this may create a very different global higher education landscape.

University rankings

With a growth in international student enrolment and research collaborations, universities around the world are increasingly placed in direct competition with one another. These competitive pressures are evident in a surge of interest in international rankings and league tables. The first international ranking of universities was issued by the Shanghai Jia Tong University Institute of Higher Education in 2003 (Knight, 2010), and it was followed in 2004 by a ranking produced by the British *Times Higher Education Supplement* and academic consulting firm Quacquarelli Symonds (Hotson, 2011). While the methods used to complete the rankings vary, they are generally based on a weighted average of the number of publications by academic staff, how often these publications are cited in other research, staff-to-student ratios and the number of doctoral degrees awarded.

Because they are such a recent development, the implications of these rankings for students, universities and governments are unclear. Their most immediate effect is to provide a global reference for comparing institutions: universities now assess their performance in relation to similar universities around the world, adding to the pressures of competition that already exist at the national level. Like rankings from international achievement tests (see Chapter 6), world university rankings are often used by national governments to legitimate policy reforms. For instance, in the United Kingdom competition with American institutions was used to support raising tuition fees (Hotson, 2011).

Criticisms of the new ranking system are manifold, starting with the basic idea they lend a false sense of objectivity to comparisons between institutions with diverse social contexts, purposes and historical backgrounds. As Marginson (2010:36) points out, global rankings are often read as a 'world's best university list' when, in fact, they are a 'research performance list'. As such, rankings favour well-funded universities, mainly in high-income countries: while institutions in low-income countries may produce more social impact with less funding, their efforts go largely unnoticed in global rankings. As the publications used to measure research impact are all written in English, predominantly English-speaking countries also have a distinct advantage (Welch, 2010). If nothing else, international rankings reflect the globalization of elite research universities. Between 2004 and 2011, the number of countries represented in *The Times* top 100 universities increased from 21 to 27 (Times Higher Education, 2004; Times Higher Education, 2011).

Reflective Exercise

- Do you think that global university rankings are reflective of academic merit?

Offshore delivery

While increasing numbers of students are going abroad for higher education (Shields and Edwards, 2010), a popular alternative is to bring the university to them, which requires new models of delivering higher education. This is done either institutionally, by creating a physical presence in foreign countries, or virtually through distance education, usually over the internet. In theory, these delivery models benefit all parties involved: students, universities and national governments. Students benefit from improved choice in higher education without the cost or inconvenience of travelling abroad. Institutions, on the other hand, are able to increase enrolment without using student spaces at their main campus. This provides additional income without depleting other revenue sources. Finally, national governments benefit from an increased supply of skilled labour and reduced 'brain drain'. While students who go abroad for their education often emigrate permanently (IOM, 2008), one can expect that those who remain in their home country are more likely to stay there after graduation.

Supported by the WTO's GATS, which contains provisions for institutions to create a 'commercial presence' in foreign countries, numerous universities have started to deliver education outside the country where they were established. The way they do so varies, and can involve anything from establishing an entirely new university to validating the teaching of local institutions. Adams (1998) provides a typology for offshore delivery models that includes branch campuses, franchising, twinning, joint degrees and distance learning.

The first model, branch campuses (sometimes called satellite campuses) involve a university setting up a physical campus in a foreign country to deliver validated degrees. According to the Observatory on Borderless Higher Education (2006), in order to qualify as a branch campus, the name of the parent university should be retained by the branch campus and degrees should be validated and awarded by the parent university. In 2009, OBHE identified at least 162 such campuses around the world; examples include the University of Nottingham in Ningbo, China; Middlesex University in Dubai; and Carnegie Mellon University in Australia (Observatory on Borderless Higher Education, 2009). Because the establishment of a branch campus can carry certain benefits to the entire country, some national governments have started programmes to attract branch campuses of prestigious universities by offering purpose-built facilities and favourable terms of taxation. Examples of this type of initiative include Qatar's Education City and Dubai's Knowledge Village.

Unlike branch campuses, franchising, twinning and joint delivery do not involve the establishment of a new campus, but rather use a partnership between universities to deliver education. Arrangements for twinning can vary considerably, and terminology is not well-standardized: the foreign institution may supply teaching material, access to teaching staff, and quality assurance; or they may simply validate existing degree programmes with a foreign 'stamp of approval' (Cavanaugh and Cavanaugh, 2006). Franchising is generally the tightest possible arrangement, as an entire degree programme that was developed by a foreign university is delivered by a local institution, with a degree being awarded by the foreign institution (HEFCE, 2011).

Finally, distance education offers the possibility to deliver higher education without any facilities or physical infrastructure whatsoever. With the rapid spread of internet access and the development of web-based Virtual Learning Environments (VLE), the delivery of online education is more feasible than at any time in the past. However, the impact of virtual delivery on the global higher education sector has been minimal, and it remains less popular than face-to-face delivery using methods described above (Shields and Edwards, 2010).

Global research networks

Just as methods of delivering higher education have become increasingly international, research conducted in universities has come to rely on global network and collaborations. It is not uncommon for researchers on opposite sides of the world to collaborate on research and the publication of scientific articles. A recent report from the Royal Society (2011) suggests that integration into global networks is essential for countries to succeed in scientific research. Like global rankings, this presents a challenge for low-income countries: participating in such networks and funding research is very expensive. Furthermore, universities in high-income countries are often able to recruit researchers from low-income countries, as they have access to better funding and facilities. The Royal Society concludes that the challenge for low-income countries is 'to reward talented scientists and enable them to foster global networks, while still using them to build national capacity' (Royal Society 2011:21). Networks between low-income countries, such as the recently established Pan Africa Chemistry Network, provide one way for universities in these countries to pool resources and undertake collaborative research on topics that are relevant to their national context (Royal Society, 2011).

The General Agreement on Trade in Services (GATS) and the liberalization of higher education

The internationalization of higher education received significant support from the WTO in its 1995 GATS. Like other WTO treaties, the primary purpose of GATS is to coordinate and promote international free trade: countries committing to the Agreement must allow all companies from foreign countries access to their markets on equal terms to local companies (Robertson, Bonal and Dale, 2002). However, GATS is very unlike other trade agreements in that it includes education as a service sector of the economy. This is in stark contrast to traditional views of education as a social service, and means that countries that agree to include their education services under GATS would allow foreign institutions (e.g. branch campuses and franchises) the right to offer degrees in competition with national universities.

Specifically, GATS stipulates that education services are one of twelve service sectors of the economy (other service sectors include tourism, health-care and financial services). Any country that allows private sector participation in its education system must also allow foreign competition. However, Verger (2009) notes that under the terms of the Agreement an institution is considered private if it charges any fees for its services, and as many public universities now charge tuition fees they could be placed in competition with foreign institutions if their national government chooses to include their education sector in GATS (Collins, 2007). To allow countries some control over the extent to which their education sector is open to free trade, GATS breaks education services into five categories that can be negotiated independently (primary, secondary, higher, adult and other education), and the following four modes of delivery:

1. Cross Border Supply: Forms of educational delivery that involve no movement of people. This comprises distance education (e.g. online study) and franchise models (see 'Branch Campuses and Alternative Delivery Models' below).
2. Consumption Abroad: Students physically going abroad for their education, also referred to as international student mobility.
3. Commercial Presence: A foreign institution opening a facility (i.e. a branch campus) in another country.
4. Presence of Natural Persons: Staff from one institution temporarily residing in another country in order to deliver educational services (WTO, 2011a).

Because it explicitly defines education as a tradable service, GATS has sparked a great deal of controversy and created a new layer of complexity for national policymakers in deciding how to fund and plan higher education. Critics of GATS (e.g. Verger, 2009) have pointed out that support for liberalizing educational services comes primarily from countries with well-developed, globally competitive higher education systems, as they stand to benefit most from exporting educational services. For low-income countries this presents something of a dilemma: there is little point in investing public funds to develop universities if they must compete with globally competitive foreign institutions; yet to deny funding for these institutions would signal a lack of support for expanding higher education. Reflecting the deep-seated resistance to GATS in many low-income countries, the Association of African Universities and UNESCO jointly issued the *Accra Declaration on GATS and the Internationalization of Higher Education in Africa* (Association of African Universities and UNESCO, 2004) which denounces 'reduction of higher education, under the GATS regime, to a tradable commodity' and 'the lack of transparency in GATS deliberations' (cited in Collins, 2006). Perhaps due to its controversial nature, many countries have been reluctant to commit educational services under GATS. To date, only 42 of the WTO's 153 member countries have committed higher education services for liberalization under GATS (WTO, 2011b).

Reflective Exercise

- Do you think that GATS has been a positive development in global higher education?

Regionalization and higher education

One broad response to the competitive pressures of the global economy has been a trend towards regionalization. Whereas in the past regionalism has been state-centric, a form of cooperation between states, this 'new regionalism' emphasizes 'the development of regions themselves as an aspect of globalization' (Tikly and Dachi, 2009:105). With a wider and more diverse economic base, regional integration offers a degree of stability and support to counteract the instability and intense competition of the global economy. This is evident in the growing influence of intergovernmental organizations that encourage intra-regional free trade, for example the European Union (EU), the Association of South East Asian Nations (ASEAN), the Economic Community of West African States (ECOWAS).

Nothing exemplifies this trend better than the creation of the European Higher Education Area, an outcome of the decade-long Bologna Process. The Bologna Process was initiated by 27 European countries in 1999 with the goal of integrating the higher education systems of European Countries (EHEA, 2010). Through a series of seven ministerial conferences, this has led to a broad standardization of undergraduate and postgraduate degrees as well as the establishment of the European Credit Transfer and Accumulation System (ECTS). The latter defines a standard system for measuring credits earned through study, so that students who study abroad or move to a university in another country can easily gain credit for their study.

By 2010, the Bologna Process had expanded to include 47 countries, reaching deep into Central Asia with the addition of Kazakhstan. This growth culminated in the formal establishment of the European Higher Education Area (EHEA) in 2010, which aims to 'ensure more comparable, compatible and coherent systems of higher education in Europe' (EHEA, 2010). There is evidence that the EHEA is already serving as a model for other regional initiatives in higher education. The ASEAN University Network recently launched the ASEAN Credit Transfer System, which is heavily based on ECTS. With evidence of similar processes taking hold in Latin America and sub-Saharan Africa (Robertson and Olds, 2011), the world of global higher education may well be a 'world of regions' (Katzenstein, 2005:174).

Summary

This chapter has discussed a set of global trends in higher education. The latter half of the twentieth century witnessed a rapid expansion of higher education globally, as well as a gradual decline in public funding for higher education and the introduction of market mechanisms. These factors created an environment that favoured internationalization; in an effort to replace lost public funding universities increasingly looked to international student enrolment and offshore delivery programmes. Internationalization resulted in other changes to the sector, such as the growing influence of international rankings and increased importance of international research networks. WTO's GATS, which defines higher education as a tradable commodity that is subject to its international free trade regulations, has played an important and controversial role in promoting the internationalization of higher education.

If these trends continue, it is possible that coming decades will see the emergence of a completely integrated, global higher education system. Universities will be cut loose from national governments and will compete to attract students from all over the world. While dramatic in nature, these changes are very recent, and there is no reason to expect that the trend towards increasing internationalization will continue. Furthermore, many of the changes associated with internationalization are built on the assumption that higher education produces economically valuable skills, which is essentially an application of human capital theory (Mincer, 1958). The internationalization of higher education depends very heavily on whether human capital theory is tenable, and the continuation of this trend is certain to put the theory to a rigorous test.

Reflective Exercise

Do you agree with following proposition:
. Individuals, not governments benefit most from higher education, and, therefore, individuals should pay for it.
In reflecting on this, you may want to consider the following:

- the importance of higher education in the 'knowledge economy' (see Chapter 6)
- the problem of 'brain drain' in low-income countries
- globalization of higher education and the new possibilities it creates
- the value of university degrees, and the intellectual autonomy of universities

Useful websites

http://iie.org/atlas – The *Atlas of Student Mobility* from the International Institute for Education. Last accessed on 4 May 2012.

www.gatswatch.org – A project to observe and analyse the effects of GATS. Last accessed on 4 May 2012.

www.obhe.ac.uk – The Observatory on Borderless Higher Education. Last accessed on 4 May 2012.

Conclusion 9

This book has shown how educational policy and practice are increasingly conceptualized and enacted on a global or international level. From the expansion of basic education to emerging trends in higher education, educational policy and practice are not determined by autonomous governments acting independently. Rather, global initiatives (e.g. the Education for All Movement – World Conference on Education for All, 1990) result from complex processes of negotiation and influence involving a web of actors at the global, regional, national and local levels. This global level of educational activity has emerged over the course of many decades and was first evident in work within international development sector following World War II. Educational activity on the global level continues to accelerate, as epitomized by the growth of international students from 1.4 million in 1998 to over 3 million in 2009 (UNESCO Institute for Statistics, 2011b).

The emergence of a global level of educational policy and practice is situated in the context of larger trends of economic and cultural convergence collectively referred to as globalization. Economically, the processes of globalization are associated with the emergence of an integrated world system: individuals' daily patterns of consumption are situated in and dependent upon an extensive network of global production, trade and finance. From a cultural perspective, globalization is associated with an 'increasing consciousness of the world as a whole' (Robertson, 1992:77) as the values and beliefs of 'modernity' take hold throughout the world. These 'world culture' values (Meyer et al., 1997) include individualism, democratic citizenship, human rights and a belief in progress. In terms of both culture and economics, education is co-constitutive of this process of economic and cultural globalization: it facilitates the transmission of world culture values and integration of individuals and societies into the world economic system, and, in turn, educational policy and practice are continually reformed and redefined by these trends.

However, it is easy to associate the rapid growth and immense reach of this global activity with a false sense of permanence and stability. This book has also shown how the emergence of significant educational activity at a global or international level has been a relatively recent phenomenon. Education in the international development sector did not begin in earnest until the 1960s, and it was not until 1990 that the conceptualization of education as a human right was supported by international commitments. Most of the growth in international student mobility has taken place only in the past ten years. It is possible that the trend of globalization will continue in coming years, that education systems will continue to converge, that integration of education systems and associated flows of people, money and ideas will increase. However, it is equally possible that the current global order will either disappear altogether or transform into something unrecognisable from its current form.

The economic preconditions of current levels of global integration are increasingly uncertain and tenuous. For example, Robertson (2005:151) quotes Immanuel Wallerstein (1999) – whose work describes the rise of an integrated world economic system over several centuries (see Chapters 1 and 5) – providing a chilling prognostication that:

> The first half of the twenty-first century will, I believe, be far more difficult, more unsettling, and yet more open than anything we have known in the twentieth century . . . the modern world system as a historical system has entered into a terminal crisis and is unlikely to exist in 50 years.

Only time will tell whether or not Wallerstein's warning of this 'terminal crisis' is accurate. However, there are many reasons to believe that the coming decades pose a formidable challenge to the current global order and the place of education within it. The financial crisis of 2008 showed that – despite its immensity – the global financial system is much more fragile and unstable than one might expect. In addition to finance, current levels of global integration are deeply dependent on abundant supplies of energy (for transportation, manufacturing and communication), yet a finite supply of fossil fuels, increasing demand from industrializing countries, population growth, and the effects of global climate change all suggest that finding that energy will not be easy as in the past (US Joint Forces Command, 2010).

The cultural norms and values that underpin global relationships are equally uncertain. Many of the principles that have guided educational activity on the global level are in flux: countries that helped to draft the Universal

Declaration of Human Rights are active or complicit in torture and international abduction (Amnesty International, 2011) while simultaneously denouncing the human rights practices in other countries as 'repressive', 'authoritarian' and 'inhumane' (US Department of State, 2011). The values and beliefs that constitute a common world culture – one that is embodied in international organizations and their declarations (Meyer et al., 1997) – appear to be more unclear than ever before. Thus, even if one disagrees with Wallerstein (1999) about the coming demise of the world system, one must nevertheless acknowledge that there are formidable challenges to be addressed if current levels of global integration are to continue.

This era of uncertainty and change creates a unique set of challenges and opportunities for research and practice in international education. Research on education must develop a coherent understanding of the complex relationship between the economic/material and cultural/institutional aspects of globalization. To date, theoretical work in this area has been largely divided. On the one hand, economic conceptualizations of globalization (i.e. Wallerstein, 1974) view the expansion of the integrated world economic system as the primary driver of globalization, viewing cultural and institutional changes as a relatively superficial artefact that reflects and perpetuates underlying economic relationships. On the other hand, cultural and institutional theories (i.e. Meyer et al., 1997), account for the prominence of international institutions and chart the diffusion of world culture values they embody (including individualism, democratic citizenship and a belief in progress), yet are remarkably silent on the divisive and contentious nature of this spread.

Research on globalization and education has the opportunity to address the tension between economic and cultural conceptualizations of globalization by focusing on the intersection of these two perspectives: the political economy of the globalization, or the nexus between material forces and cultural practices. Education is a key element of this political economy, as educational policy and practice are integral to both economic and cultural activity. The intersection of economic and cultural aspects of globalization can be studied in many specific contexts, including those discussed in this book, but also in emerging areas such global citizenship education, and education for sustainable development (see below). Future research on education and globalization should further investigate how material/economic and cultural/institutional factors relate to one another, and what this says about the processes of globalization.

A better understanding of the political economy of globalization and education also opens up possibilities for practice that redefines the conditions of globalization in a way that averts the possibility of Wallerstein's (1999) terminal crisis. Foundations for such changes are already present: for example, the United Nations formally declared the years 2005–14 as the 'Decade of Education for Sustainable Development', with a goal of preparing 'people of all walks of life to . . . find solutions for issues that threaten the sustainability of our planet' (UNESCO, 2005b). While such initiatives embody lofty goals, it remains to be seen whether they will be successful in effecting substantive change. To create a truly sustainable society would necessitate major reforms, and such changes would upset the advantages enjoyed by economically powerful groups (e.g. large companies that rely on environmental exploitation to make profits). Rather than resisting the move towards sustainability altogether (which would be untenable within the framework of world culture values), economic interests may seek to co-opt this movement into something more tokenistic, paying lip-service to pressing issues while actually resulting in little change. This illustrates the political economy of globalization at work: institutions such as UNESCO embody world culture values, yet they are also susceptible to influence from economic interests that seek to redefine these values in a way that serves their goals.

To distinguish between genuine reform efforts and those that co-opt the discourse of reform to legitimate the status quo requires strong critical analysis and skills. The ability to make this distinction is part of what Freire (1970:8) terms 'critical consciousness', the independent analysis of social relationships of power and oppression that results in informed action. Development of critical consciousness through education is difficult; not only does it require an innovative and interactive pedagogy, but it often involves defying authority and unseating vested interests. However, if integrated educational work on a global level is to continue, development of critical consciousness through education is a vital necessity and a worthy goal.

Reflective Exercise

- Do you think that global connectivity, integration and convergence will continue to increase in coming decades?

Appendix: International Education and Development Timeline

1944 – Bretton Woods Conference establishes the World Bank, which goes on to become a major development donor.

1945 – The United Nations Charter is signed by 50 original member countries.

1946 – Both UNESCO and UNICEF are founded.

1947 – India gains independence, the first major colony to become independent in the twentieth century. This marks the beginning of the end of the British Empire.

1948 – The United Nations' Universal Declaration of Human Rights is ratified by a 48–0 vote, with eight abstentions. Among other things, it declares that 'Everyone has the Right to Education'.

1960 – The United Nations declares 1960–1970 as the 'Development Decade'.

1960 – Most French colonies in Africa gain independence, including Senegal, Niger, Mali, Chad, Cameroon and Burkina Faso.

1960 – W. W. Rostow's *Stages of Economic Growth: A Non-Communist Manifesto* is published.

1960 – World Bank founds its International Development Association (IDA) – a special branch of the organization devoted to financing projects in developing countries.

1961 – The United States Agency of International Development (USAID) is founded.

1963 – The World Bank makes its first loan for education.

1964 – The United Kingdom's ministry of Overseas Development is founded. In 1997 it is renamed the Department for International Development (DFID).

1965 – The United Nations starts the United Nations Development Programme (UNDP).

1970 – The United Nations declares 1970–1980 as the 'Second Development Decade'.

1980 – Zimbabwe, the last major British Colony, gains independence.

1980 – World Bank begins Structural Adjustment Programmes.

1990 – The World Conference on Education for All is held in Jomtien, Thailand. It pledges to universalise basic education by the year 2000.

2000 – UN Summit on the Millennium Development Goals adopts eight global goals to achieve by 2015.

2000 – World Education Forum meets in Dakar, Senegal and extends the EFA deadline to 2015.

2008 – The EFA midterm review finds that global net enrolment is 87 per cent, with 72 million children not in school.

2015 – Deadline for the Millennium Development Goals and Dakar Framework for Action to achieve Education for All.

Bibliography

50x15 Foundation. (2010). Partners. Retrieved from http://50x15.org/partners. Last accessed on 25 October 2010.

Abbott, G. C. (1971). 'A re-examination of the 1929 Colonial Development Act'. *The Economic History Review*, 24(1), 68–81.

Ablett, J. et al. (2007). *The 'Bird of. Gold:' the Rise of India's Consumer Market*. McKinsey Global Institute.

Ackerman, E. (2001). Piaget's constructivism, Papert's constructionism: what's the difference? *Constructivism: uses and perspectives in education, Vols 1 and 2*, Conference Proceedings, Geneva, Research Centre in Education, 85–94.

Adams, T. (1998). 'The operation of transnational degree and diploma programs: The Australian case'. *Journal of Studies in International Education*, 2(3), 3–22.

Ahmed, A. U., and M. Arends-Kuennig. (2006). 'Do crowded classrooms crowd out learning? Evidence from the food for education program in Bangladesh'. *World Development*, 34(4), 665–84.

Altbach, P. G. (2004) 'Globalization and the university'. *Tertiary Education and Management*, 10, 3–25.

Álvarez-Mendiola, G. (2006). 'Lifelong learning policies in Mexico: context, challenges and comparisons'. *Compare: A Journal of Comparative and International Education*, 36(3), 379–99.

Amnesty International. (2011) *Guantánamo: A Decade of Damage to Human Rights*. Index: AMR 51/103/2011. London: Amnesty International.

Anderson, J. (2011). 'From Finland, a story of educational success in going against the tide'. *The New York Times*, 13 December, p. A33.

Anwer, J. (2012). IIT Rajasthan caused failure of Aakash I: Datawind. Retrieved from http://timesofindia. indiatimes.com/business/india-business/IIT-Rajasthan-caused-failure-of-Aakash-I-Datawind/ articleshow/12540744.cms. Last accessed on 5 April 2012.

Archer, D. (2004). 'NGO Perspectives on adult literacy'. *Convergence*, 37(3), 65–74.

Arnove, R. F. (1980). 'Comparative education and world-systems analysis'. *Comparative Education Review*, 24(1), 48–62.

—. (1999). 'Introduction to "Reframing comparative education: The dialectic of the global and the local"'. In R. F. Arnove and C. A. Torres (eds), *Comparative Education: The Dialectic of the Global and the Local*. Lanham, MD: Rowman and Littlefield Publishers, pp. 1–20.

—. (2009). 'World-systems analysis and comparative education in an age of globalization'. In R. Cowen and A. M. Kazamias (eds), *International Handbook of Comparative Education* (Vol. Two). New York: Springer, pp. 101–20.

Association of African Universities and UNESCO (2004). Accra Declaration on GATS and the Internationalization of Higher Education in Africa. Signed at the Workshop on the Implications of WTO/GATS for Higher Education in Africa, Accra, Ghana, 29 April.

Astiz, M. F., A. W. Wiseman and D. P. Baker. (2002). 'Slouching towards decentralization: consequences of globalization for curricular control in national education systems'. *Comparative Education Review*, 46(1), 66–88.

Barnett, G. A. and R. Y. Wu. (1995). 'The international student exchange network: 1970 & 1989'. *Higher Education*, 30(4), 353–68.

Barrera-Osorio, F., T. Fasih and H. A. Patrinos. (2009). *Decentralized Decision-Making in Schools: The Theory and Evidence on School-Based Management*. Washington, DC: World Bank.

Bassett, T. J. and Winter-Nelson, A. (2010). *The Atlas of World Hunger*. Chicago: University of Chicago Press.

Bassey, M. O. (1999). *Western Education and Political Domination in Africa*. London: Bergin and Garvey.

BBC. (2010). India unveils prototype for $35 touch-screen computer. 23 July 2010. Retrieved from www.bbc.co.uk/news/world-south-asia-10740817. Last accessed on 31 January 2012.

Beckfield, J. (2010). 'The social structure of the world polity'. *American Journal of Sociology*, 115(4), 1018–68.

Bell, D. (1974). *The Coming of Post-Industrial Society: A Venture in Social Forecasting*. London: Heinemann.

Benavot, A. and P. Riddle. (1988). 'The expansion of primary education, 1870–1940: trends and issues'. *Sociology of Education*, 61, 191–210.

Bereday, G. Z. F. (1957). 'Discussion of methods in comparative education'. *Comparative Education Review*, 1(1), 13–15.

Boli, J. and M. G. Thomas. (1997). 'World culture in the world polity: a century of international non-governmental organization'. *American Sociological Review*, 62(2), 171–90.

Boli, J., F. O. Ramirez and J. W. Meyer. (1985). 'Explaining the origins and expansion of mass education'. *Comparative Education Review*, 29(2), 145–70.

Böhm, A. A. Böhm, M. Follari, A. Hewett, S. Jones, N. Kemp, D. Meares, D. Pearce and K. Van Cauter (2004). *Vision 2020: Forecasting International Student Mobility: A UK Perspective*. London: British Council.

Borrás, S. (2009). 'The politics of the Lisbon Strategy: the changing role of the Commission'. *West European Politics*, 32(1), 97–118.

Bowles, S. and H. Gintis. (1976). *Schooling in Capitalist America: Educational Reform and the Contradictions of Economic Life*. New York: Basic Books.

Bray, H. (2009). 'Cheaper cheap laptop promised'. *The Boston Globe*, 11 February.

Bray, M. (1996). *Decentralisation of Education: Community Financing*. Washington, DC: World Bank.

—. (2003). 'Comparative education in the era of globalization: evolution, mission and roles'. *Policy Futures in Education*, 1(2), 209–24.

Brock-Utne, B. (2000). *Whose Education for All: The Recolonization of the African Mind*. New York: Falmer Press.

—. (2001). 'Education for all – in whose language?' *Oxford Review of Education*, 27(1), 115–34.

Bromley, P. and M. Andina. (2010). 'Standardizing chaos: a neo-institutional analysis of the INEE Minimum Standards for Education in Emergencies, chronic crises and early reconstruction'. *Compare: A Journal of Comparative and International Education*, 40(5), 575–88.

Brown, P. and H. Lauder. (2006). 'Globalisation, knowledge and the myth of the magnet economy'. *Globalisation, Societies and Education*, 4(1), 25–57.

Brown, P., H. Lauder and D. Ashton. (2011). *The Global Auction: The Broken Promises of Education, Job and, Incomes*. Oxford: Oxford University Press.

Bryan, A. (2008). 'Researching and searching for international development in the formal curriculum: Towards a post-colonial conceptual framework'. *Policy and Practice: A Development Education Review*, 7(1), 68–79.

Buckland, P. (2005). *Reshaping the Future: Education and Post-Conflict Reconstruction*. Washington, DC: World Bank.

Burde, D. (2004). 'International NGOs and best practices: the art of educational lending'. In G. Steiner-Khamsi (ed.), *The Global Politics of Educational Borrowing and Lending*. New York: Teachers College Press, pp. 173–88.

Bush, K. D. and D. Saltarelli. (2000). *The Two Faces of Education in Ethnic Conflict: Towards a Peacebuilding Education for Children*. Florence: UNICEF.

Caddell, M. (2002). *Outward Looking Eyes: Visions of Schooling, Development and the State in Nepal*. Unpublished DPhil dissertation. Edinburgh: University of Edinburgh.

Carney, S. (2009). 'Negotiating policy in an age of globalization: exploring educational policyscapes in Nepal, Denmark and China'. *Comparative Education Review*, 53(1), 63–88.

—. (2010). 'Reading the global: comparative education at the end of an era'. In M. Larsen (ed.), *New Thinking in Comparative Education: Honouring the Work of Dr. Robert Cowen*. Rotterdam: Sense Publishers, pp. 125–42.

Carney, S. and M. B. Bista (2009). Community schooling in Nepal: a genealogy of reform since 1990'. *Comparative Education Review*, 53(2), 189–211.

Carney, S. and J. Rappleye. (2011). 'Education reform in Nepal: from modernity to conflict'. *Globalisation, Societies and Education*, 9(1), 1–9.

Carnoy, M., R. Jacobsen, L. Mishel and R. Rothstein. (2005). *The charter school dust-up: Examining the evidence on enrollment and achievement*. New York: Teachers College Press.

—. (2006). 'The charter school dust-up: examining the evidence on enrolment and achievement'. *Teachers College Record*, 108(5), 869–72.

Cavanaugh, J. C. and C. K. Cavanaugh. (2006). 'Franchising higher education'. *Chronicle of Higher Education: The Chronicle Review*, 52(33), 21 April: B20.

Chiriyankandath, J. (2011). 'Colonialism and post-colonial development'. In P. Burnell, V. Randall and L. Rakner (eds) *Politics in the Developing World* (3rd edn). Oxford: Oxford University Press, pp. 35–52.

Clayton, T. (2004). '"Competing conceptions of globalization" revisited: relocating the tension between world-systems analysis and globalization analysis'. *Comparative Education Review*, 48(3), 274–94.

Coleman, J. S. (1958). *Nigeria: Background to Nationalism*. Berkeley: University of California Press.

Collier, P. (2007). *The Bottom Billion: Why the Poorest Countries are Failing and What Can Be Done About It*. Oxford: Oxford University Press.

Collins, C. S. (2007). 'A general agreement on higher education: GATS, globalization, and imperialism'. *Research in Comparative and International Education*, 2(4), 283–96.

Correa, C. M. (2001). 'The TRIPS agreement, how much room for manoeuvre?' *Journal of Human Development*, 2(1), 79–107.

Cuban, L. (2001). *Oversold and Underused: Computers in the Classroom*. Cambridge, MA: Harvard University Press.

D'Aeth, R. (1975). *Education and Development in the Third World*. Westmead: Saxon House.

Darling-Hammond, L. (2011). U.S. versus highest-achieving nations in education. Retrieved from http://bit.ly/educachieve. Last accessed on 12 September 2012.

Davies, L. (2004). *Education and Conflict: Complexity and Chaos*. London: Routledge Falmer.

—. (2005). 'Schools and war: urgent agendas for comparative and international education'. *Compare: A Journal of Comparative and International Education*, 35(4), 357–71.

—. (2010). 'The different faces of education in conflict'. *Development*, 53(4), 491–7.

Deaton, A. and Kozel, V. (2005). Data and dogma: The great Indian poverty debate. *The World Bank Research Observer*, 20(2), 177–99.

Department for Business, Innovation and Skills. (2009). *Higher Ambition: The Future of Universities in a Knowledge Economy*. London: Author.

Department for Education (UK). (2010). Funding for primary and service children's education schools. Retrieved from www.education.gov.uk/aboutdfe/foi/disclosuresaboutschools/a0068115/. Last accessed on 31 January 2012.

Department for International Development. (2000). *Eliminating World Poverty: Making Globalisation Work for the Poor*. White Paper on International Development. London: Author.

DeVoe, J. E. et al. (2007). Insurance plus access does not equal health care: Typology of barriers to health care access for low-income families. *Annals of Family Medicine*, 5(6), 511–18.

DFID. (2001). Imfundo: Partnership of IT in Education. Inception Report. London: DFID.

—. (2012). Where we work. Retrieved from: http://www.dfid.gov.uk/Where-we-work/. Last accessed on 10 September 2012.

Drucker, P. (1968). *The Age of Discontinuity: Guidelines to Our Changing Society*. New York: Harper & Row.

Economist, The. (2009). China is number one: more than a billion people are using the internet. *The Economist*, 26 January 2009. Retrieved from www.economist.com/node/13007996. Last accessed on 31 January 2012.

Edwards, A. (2012). *New Technology and Education*. London: Continuum.

Edwards, R. M. (2011). 'Disconnect and capture of education decentralisation reforms in Nepal: implications for community involvement in schooling'. *Globalisation, Societies and Education*, 9(1), 67–84.

EHEA. (2010). *Towards the European Union Higher Education Area*. Vienna: Austrian Federal Ministry of Science and Research.

Escobar, A. (1995). *Encountering Development: The Making and Unmaking of the Third World*. Princeton: Princeton University Press.

European Council. (2000). Lisbon European Council: presidency conclusions. Retrieved from www. europarl.europa.eu/summits/lis1_en.htm. Last accessed on 31 January 2012.

Fairclough, N. (1995). *Critical Discourse Analysis: The Critical Study of Language*. New York: Longman.

Feder, B. J. (2006). 'Theodore Levitt, 81, who coined the term "globalization," is dead'. *New York Times*, 6 July. Business Section.

Ferguson, J. (1990). *The Anti-Politics Machine: 'Development,' Depoliticization and Bureaucratic Power in Lesotho*. Cambridge: Cambridge University Press.

Fleck, R.K. and C. Kilby. (2006). How do political changes influence US bilateral aid allocations? Evidence from panel data. *Review of Development Economics*, 10(2), 210–23.

Forshay, A. W., R. L. Thorndike, F. Hotyat, D. A. Pidgeon and D. A. Walker. (1962). *Educational Achievements of Thirteen-Year-Olds in Twelve Countries*. Hamburg: UNESCO Institute for Education.

Foucault, M. (1975). *Discipline and Punish: The Birth of the Prison*. Translated by Alan Sheridan. London: Penguin Books.

Fraser, A. (2009). Zambia: Back to the future? In L. Whitfield (ed.), *The Politics of Aid: African Strategies for Dealing with Donors*. Oxford: Oxford University Press, 299–328.

Freire, P. (1970). *Pedagogy of the Oppressed*. New York: Continuum.

Friedman, T. L. (2000) *The Lexus and the Olive Tree*. New York: First Anchor Press.

—. (2006). *The World is Flat: A Brief History of the Twenty-First Century*. New York: Farrar, Straus and Giroux.

Gallego, F. A. (2010). 'Historical origins of schooling: the role of democracy and political decentralization'. *The Review of Economics and Statistics*, 92(2), 228–43.

Geng, Y. and B. Doberstein. (2008). 'Developing the circular economy in China: challenges and opportunities for achieving "leapfrog development"'. *International Journal of Sustainable Development and World Ecology*, 15, 231–9.

Giddens, A. (1999). *Runaway World: How Globalisation is Reshaping Our Lives*. London: Profile Books.

Giddens, A. (2000). *The Third Way and Its Critics*. Cambridge: Blackwell Publishers Ltd.

Goodson, I. F. and J. M. Mangan. (1996). Computer literacy as ideology. *British Journal of Sociology of Education*, 17(1), 65–79.

Gosh, S. C. (2007). *History of Education in India*. Jaipur: Rawat Publications.

Gove, M. (2010). 'PISA slip should put a rocket under our world-class ambitions and drive us to win the education space race'. *Times Educational Supplement*, 17 December.

Grek, S. (2009). 'Governing by numbers: the PISA "effect" in Europe'. *Journal of Education Policy*, 24(1), 23–37.

Gunter, H. (2011). Introduction: Contested educational reform. In H. Gunter (ed.), *The State and Education Policy: The Academies Programme*. London: Continuum, 1–18.

Gürüz, K. (2008). *Higher Education and International Student Mobility in the Global Knowledge Economy*. Albany: State University of New York Press.

Hagan, J. and J. Kaiser. (2011). 'The displaced and dispossessed of Darfur: explaining the sources of a continuing state-led genocide'. *British Journal of Sociology*, 62(1), 1–25.

Ham, S-W. and Y-K. Cha. (2009). 'Positioning education in the information society: the transnational diffusion of the information and communication technology curriculum'. *Comparative Education Reivew*, 59(4), 535–57.

Heeks, R. (1996). *India's Software Industry: State Policy, Liberalisation and Industrial Development*. Delhi: Sage Publications India.

Heidelberg Institute for International Conflict Research. (2009). 'Conflict Barometer 2009'. Heidelberg: University of Heidelberg.

Herz, B. and G. B. Sperling. (2004). *What Works in Girls' Education: Evidence and Policies from the Developing World*. New York: Council on Foreign Relations.

Higher Education Funding Council for England. (2011). Glossary: franchise. Retrieved from www.hefce.ac.uk/aboutus/glossary/glossary.htm. Last accessed on 31 January 2012.

Hill, D. J. (2007). *Hegemony and Education: Gramsci, Post-Marxism, and Radical Democracy Revisited*. Lanham: Lexington Books.

Holmes, B. (1981). *Comparative Education: Some Considerations of Method*. London: Unwin Education Books.

Hotson, H. (2011). 'Don't look to the Ivy League'. *London Review of Books*, 33(10), 20–22.

Huntington, S. P. (1997). *The Clash of Civilizations and the Remaking of World Order*. New York: Simon and Schuster.

Illich, I. D. (1971). *Deschooling Society*. New York: Harper and Row.

Inaugural Addresses of the Presidents of the United States, vol. 2. (2009). Bedford, Massachusetts: Applewood Books.

INEE. (2004). Minimum Standards for Education in Emergencies, Chronic Crisis and Early Reconstruction. Paris: INEE.

International Organization for Migration. (2008). *World Migration 2008*. Geneva: Author.

ITU. (2012). Key global telecom indicators for the world telecommunication service sector. Retrieved from: http://www.itu.int/ITU-D/ict/statistics/at_glance/KeyTelecom.html.Last accessed on 11 September 2012.

Jackson, P. W. (1968). *Life in Classrooms*. New York: Holt, Rinehart and Winston.

James, J. (2003). *Bridging the Global Digital Divide*. Cheltenham: Edward Elgar Publishing.

Jessop, B. (2002). *The Future of the Capitalist State*. London: Polity Press.

Jimenez, E. and Y. Sawada. (1998). 'Do community managed schools work? An evaluation of El Salvador's EDUCO program'. *Working Paper Series on Impact Evaluation of Education Reforms*, Number 8. Washington, DC: World Bank.

Jones, P. W. (2004). 'Taking the credit: financing and policy linkages in the education portfolio of the World Bank'. In G. Steiner-Khamsi (ed.), *The Global Politics of Educational Borrowing and Lending*. New York: Teachers College Press, pp. 188–200.

—. (2006). *Education, Poverty and the World Bank*. Rotterdam: Sense Publishers.

Jørgensen, M. and J. P. Phillips. (2002). *Discourse Analysis as Theory and Method*. London: Sage Publications.

Kagawa, F. (2005). 'Emergency education: a critical review of the field'. *Comparative Education*, 41(4), 487–503.

Kaldor, M. (1998). *New Wars and Old Wars: Organized Violence in a Global Era*. Cambridge, UK: Polity Press.

Kandel, I. L. (1935). *Studies in Comparative Education*. London: George G. Harrap.

Kapur, D., J. P. Lewis and R. C. Webb. (1997). *The World Bank: Its First Half-Century*. Volume 1. Washington, DC: The Brookings Institution.

Karkaria, R. P. (1907). *Lord Curzon's Farewell to India: Being Speeches Delivered As Viceroy and Governor General of India*. Mumbai: Thacker and Company.

Katzenstein, P. J. (2005). *A World of Regions: Asia and Europe in the American Imperium*. Ithaca: Cornell University Press.

Kelly, M. J. (1991). *Education in a Declining Economy: The case of Zambia 1975 –1985*. Washington, DC: World Bank.

Kimura, I. (2003). *Goals and Roles of Basic Education in Human Development – Case: Bangladesh*. Unpublished doctoral dissertation. University of California, Los Angeles.

Klees, S. (2001). 'World Bank development policy: a SAP in SWAPs clothing'. *Current Issues in Comparative Education*, 3(2), 110–21.

Knight, J. (2010). 'Internationalization and the competitiveness agenda'. In V. D. Rust, L. M. Portnoi, and S. S. Bagley (eds), *Higher Education, Policy, and the Global Competition Phenomenon*. New York: Palgrave Macmillan, pp. 205–18.

Kuznetsov, Y. and C. Dahlman. (2008). *Mexico's Transition to a Knowledge-Based Economy: Challenges and Opportunities*. Washington, DC: World Bank.

Lai-ngok, J. W. (2004). 'School autonomy in China: a comparison between government and private schools within the context of decentralization'. *International Studies in Educational Administration*, 32(3), 58–73.

Lingard, B. and K. D. Jn Pierre. (2006). 'Strengthening national capital: a postcolonial analysis of lifelong learning policy in St Lucia, Caribbean'. *Pedagogy, Culture and Society*, 14(3), 295–314.

Love, R. (2007). 'Corporate wealth or public health? WTO/TRIPS flexibilities and access to HIV/AIDS antiretroviral drugs by developing countries'. *Development in Practice*, 17(2), 208–19.

Lugaz, C. and A. De Grauwe. (2010). *Schooling and Decentralization: Patterns and Policy Implications in Francophone West Africa*. Paris: UNESCO International Institute for Educational Planning.

Machlup, F. (1962). The Production and Distribution of Knowledge in the United States. Princeton: Princeton University Press.

Marginson, S. (2010). 'Global comparisons and the university knowledge economy'. In V. D. Rust, L. M. Portnoi and S. S. Bagley (eds), *Higher Education, Policy, and the Global Competition Phenomenon*. New York: Palgrave Macmillan, pp. 29–42.

Mehrotra, S. (1998). 'Education for all: policy lessons from high-achieving countries'. *International Review of Education*, 5(6), 461–84.

Meyer, J. W., J. Boli, G. M. Thomas and F. Ramirez. (1997). 'World society and the nation state'. *American Journal of Sociology*, 103(1), 144–81.

Miller-Grandvaux, Y. (2002). *A Literature Review of Community Schools in Africa*. Washington, DC: Academy for Educational Development.

Mincer, J. (1958). 'Investment in human capital and personal income distribution'. *The Journal of Political Economy*, 66, 281–382.

Mitra, S. (2003). Minimally invasive education: a progress report on the "hole-in-the-wall" experiments. *British Journal of Educational Technology*, 34(3), 367–71.

Mohanty, C. (1991). *Third World Women and the Politics of Feminism*. Bloomington: Indiana University Press.

Morrison, K. (2002). *School Leadership and Complexity Theory*. London: Routledge Falmer.

Moyi, P. (2012). 'Who goes to school? School enrolment patterns in Somalia'. *International Journal of Educational Development*, 32(1), 163–71.

Mullikottu-Veettil, M. and M. Bray. (2004). 'The decentralisation of education in Kerala state, India: rhetoric and reality'. *International Review of Education*, 50, 223–43.

Mullis, I. V. S., M. O. Martin, D. F. Robitaille and P. Foy. (2009a). *TIMSS Advanced 2008 International Report*. Boston: TIMSS & PIRLS International Study Centre.

Mullis, I. V. S., M. O. Martin, G. J. Ruddock, C. Y. O'Sullivan and C. Preuschoff. (2009b). *TIMSS 2011 Assessment Frameworks*. Boston: TIMSS & Pirls International Study Centre.

Murphy, C. N. (2006). *The United Nations Development Programme: A Better Way*? Cambridge: Cambridge University Press.

National Science Teachers Assocation. (2010). *National Lab Day: A National Barn-Raising for Hands-On Learning*. Arlington: Author.

Negroponte, N. (2007). 'One laptop per child, two years on'. *The Entertainment Gathering (TED)*, 2–4 December 2007, Los Angeles, CA.

Nepal Education Planning Commission. (1956). *Education in Nepal: Report of the Nepal National Education Planning Commission*. Kathmandu, Nepal: Bureau of Publications, College of Education.

Noah, H. J. (2006). Video-recorded interview. In G. Steiner-Khamsi and E. M. Johnson, producers, *Comparative Speaking: An Oral History of the First 50 Years of the Comparative and International Education Society*. New York: Teacher's College, Columbia University.

Novelli, M. (2010). 'Education, conflict and social (in)justice: insights from Colombia'. *Educational Review*, 62(3), 271–85.

Novelli, M. and Cardozo, M. T. A. L. (2008). 'Conflict, education and the global south: new critical directions'. *International Journal of Educational Development*, 28, 473–88.

Novoa, A. (1998). *Histoire et Comparaison (Essais sur l'éducation)*. Lisbonne: Educa.

Observatory on Borderless Higher Education. (2006). *The International Branch Campus: Models and Trends*. London: Author.

—. (2009). *International Branch Campuses: Markets & Strategies*. London: Author.

OECD. (2000). *Measuring Student Knowledge and Skills: the PISA 2000 Assessment of Reading, Mathematical and Scientific Literacy*. Paris: Author.

—. (2009). *Assessment Framework: Key Competencies in Reading, Mathematics and Science*. Paris: Author.

OLPC. (2011). Mission. Retrieved from http://laptop.org/en/vision/mission. Last accessed on 31 January 2012.

Off, C. (2004). Back to school in Afghanistan. *CBC News*. Retrieved from www.cbc.ca/news/background/afghanistan/schools.html. Last accessed on 31 January 2012

Owen, D. (1959). 'The United Nations Expanded Program of Technical Assistance: a multilateral approach. *Annals of the American Academic of Political and Social Science*, 323, 25–32.

Papert, S. (1980). *Mindstorms: Children, Computers and Powerful Ideas*. New York: Basic Books.

—. (1993). *The Children's Machine: Rethinking School in the Age of the Computer*. New York: Basic Books.

Parker, S. and K. Standing. (2007). 'The impact of conflict on schooling in Nepal'. In F. Leach and M. Dunne (eds), *Education, Conflict and Reconciliation: International Perspectives*. Bern: Peter Lang, pp. 51–64.

Paulson, J. (2008). 'The two faces today?' *Research in Comparative and International Education*, 3(1), 1–4.

—. (2011). 'Reconciliation through educational reform? Recommendations and realities in Peru'. In J. Paulson (ed.), *Education and Reconciliation: Exploring Conflict and Post-Conflict Situations*. London: Continuum, pp. 126–50.

Paulson, J. and J. Rappleye. (2007). 'Education and conflict: essay review'. *International Journal of Educational Development*, 27, 340–47.

Pearce, K. C. (2001). *Rostow, Kennedy and the Rhetoric of Foreign Aid*. East Lansing: Michigan State University Press.

Pherali, T. (2011). 'Education and conflict in Nepal: possibilities for reconstruction'. *Globalisation, Societies and Education*, 9(1), 135–54.

Phillips, D. and M. Schweisfurth. (2008) *Comparative and International Education: An Introduction to Theory, Method and Practice*. Oxford: Continuum.

Phillips, L. and M. W. Jørgenson. (2002). *Discourse Analysis as Theory and Method*. London: Sage Publications.

Pigg, S. L. (1992) 'Inventing social categories through place: social representations and development in Nepal'. *Comparative Studies in Society and History*, 34(3), 491–513.

Portnoi, L. M., S. S. Bagley and V. D. Rust. (2010). Mapping the terrain: The global competition phenomenon in higher education. In V. D. Rust, L. M. Portnoi, and S. S. Bagley (eds), *Higher Education, Policy, and the Global Competition Phenomenon*. New York: Palgrave Macmillan, pp. 1–13.

Pratt-Adams, S., M. Maguire and E. Burn. (2010). *Changing Urban Education*. London: Continuum.

Prensky, M. (2001). 'Digital natives, digital immigrants'. Part 1. *On the Horizon*, 9(5), 1–6.

Presbich, R. (1959). 'Commercial policy in the underdeveloped countries'. *American Economic Review*, 49(2), 251–73.

Rappleye, J. (2011a). 'Catalysing educational development or institutionalising external influence? Donors, civil society and educational policy formation in Nepal'. *Globalisation, Societies and Education*, 9(1), 27–49.

—. (2011b). 'Different presumptions about progress, different prescriptions for peace. connections between conflict, development and education in Nepal'. In J. Paulson (ed.) *Education, Conflict and Development*. Oxford: Symposium Books, pp. 59–100.

Rahman, A. A., Alam, M. Alam, S. S. Uzzaman, M. R., Rashid, M. and Rabbani, G. (2007). UN Human Development Report 2007: Background Paper on Risks, vulnerability and adaptation in Bangladesh. Dhaka: Bangladesh Centre for Advanced Studies.

Rhoten, D. (2000). 'Education decentralization in Argentina: a "global-local conditions of possibility" approach to state, market, and society change'. *Journal of Education Policy*, 15(6), 593–619.

Riddell, R. C. (2007). *Does Foreign Aid Really Work?* Oxford: Oxford University Press.

Roberstson, R. (1992). *Globalization: Social Theory and Global Culture*. London: Sage Publications.

Robertson, S. L. (2005). 'Re-imagining and rescripting the future of education: global knowledge economy discourses and the challenge to education systems'. *Comparative Education*, 41(2), 151–70.

—. (2011). 'Reconceptualising "state space" in the globalisation and governance of education policy'. Presented at the annual conference of the Comparative and International Education Society, 1–5 May 2011, Montreal, Canada.

Robertson, S. L. and K. Olds. (2011). 'Global regionalisms and higher education: mapping projects, challenging concepts'. Paper presented at the Observatory on Borderless Higher Education Global Forum, 25–27 May, Vancouver.

Robertson, S. L., X. Bonal and R. Dale. (2002). 'GATS and the education service Industry: the politics of scale and global reterritorialization'. *Comparative Education Review*, 46(4), 472–96.

Rose, P. (2005). 'Is there a "fast track" to achieving education for all?' *International Journal of Educational Development*, 25, 381–94.

Rostow, W. W. (1960). *The Stages of Economic Growth: A Non-Communist Manifesto.* Cambridge: Cambridge University Press.

Royal Society. (2011). *Knowledge, Networks and Nations: Global Scientific Collaboration in the Twentieth Century*. London: Author.

Rutayisire, J. (2007). 'The role of teachers in the social and political reconstruction of post-genocide Rwanda'. In F. Leach and M. Dunne (eds), *Education, Conflict and Reconciliation: International Perspectives*. Bern: Peter Lang, pp. 115–30.

Sachs, J. D. (2005). *The End of Poverty: The Economic Possibilities of Our Time*. New York: Penguin Press.

Said, E. W. (1978). *Orientalism*. New York: Vintage Books.

Salmi, J. (2009). *The Challenge of Establishing World-Class Universities*. Washington, DC: World Bank.

Samoff, J. (2004). From funding projects to supporting sectors? Observations on the aid relationship in Burkina Faso. *International Journal of Educational Development*, 24, 397–427.

Schofer, E. and J. W. Meyer. (2005). 'The worldwide expansion of higher education in the twentieth century'. *American Sociological Review*, 70, 898–920.

Schooling the World: The Whiteman's Last Burden. (2011). Directed by Carol Black.

Schramm. W. (1964). *Mass Media and National Development: The Role of Information in the Developing Countries*. Stanford: Stanford University Press.

Schweisfurth, M. (2006). 'Global and cross-national influences on education in post-genocide Rwanda'. *Oxford Review of Education*, 32(5), 697–709.

Sen, A. (1983). 'Development: Which way now?' *The Economic Journal*, 93, 745–62.

—. (1999). *Development as Freedom*. New York: Anchor Books.

Senzaki, N. (1919/2010). *101 Zen Stories*. Whitefish, Montana: Kessinger Publishing (Reprint).

Shahjahan, R. A. (2011). 'Decolonizing the evidence–based education and policy movement: revealing the colonial vestiges in educational policy, research, and neoliberal reform'. *Journal of Education Policy*, 26(2), 181–206.

Shields, R. (2005). 'Political conflict and schooling in Nepal: teacher attitudes and coping mechanisms'. Paper presented to the Comparative and International Education Society Annual Conference, Honolulu, Hawaii, 15 March.

—. (2009). The landlocked island: information access and communications policy in Nepal. *Telecommunications Policy*, 33(3), 207–14.

—. (2011). 'ICT or I see tea? Modernity, technology and education in Nepal'. *Globalisation, Societies and Education*, 9(1), 85–97.

Shields, R. and R. Edwards. (2010). 'Student mobility and emerging hubs in global higher education'. In V. D. Rust, L. M. Portnoi and S. S. Bagley (eds), *Higher Education, Policy, and the Global Competition Phenomenon*. New York: Palgrave Macmillan, pp. 235–8.

Shields, R. and J. Rappleye. (2008a). 'Uneven terrain: educational policy and equity in Nepal'. *Asia Pacific Journal of Education*, 28(3), 265–76.

—. (2008b). 'Differentiation, development, (dis)integration: education in Nepal's "People's War"'. *Research in Comparative and International Education*, 3(1), 91–102.

Shiva, V. (1989). *The Violence of the Green Revolution: Ecological degradation and political conflict in Punjab*. Dehra Dun: Author.

Simutanyi, N. (1996). 'The politics of structural adjustment in Zambia'. *Third World Quarterly*, 17(4), 825–39.

Sinclair, M. (2001). 'Education in emergencies'. In J. Crisp, C. Talbot and D. B. Cipollone (eds), *Learning for a Future: Refugee Education in Developing Countries*. Geneva: United Nations High Commissioner for Refugees, pp. 1–84.

Sklair, L. (1999). 'Competing conceptualizations of globalization'. *Journal of World-Systems Research*, 2, 143–63.

Smith, A. (1776/1999). *The Wealth of Nations. Books I – III*. Edited by Andrew Skinner. London: Penguin Books.

Spring, J. (2008). *Globalization and Education: An Introduction*. New York: Routledge.

Stambach, A. and G. A. Malekea. (2006). 'Education, technology, and the "new" knowledge economy: views from Bongoland'. *Globalisation, Societies and Education*, 4(3), 321–36.

Steiner-Khamsi, G. (2004a). 'Blazing a trail for policy theory and practice'. In G. Steiner-Khamsi (ed.), *The Global Politics of Educational Borrowing and Lending*. New York: Teachers College Press, pp. 201–20.

—. (2004b). 'Globalization in Education: Real or Imagined?' In G. Steiner-Khamsi (ed.), *The Global Politics of Educational Borrowing and Lending*. New York: Teachers College Press, pp. 1–6.

Stephens, J. and D. B. Ottoway. (2002). 'From U.S., the ABC's of jihad: violent Soviet-era textbooks complicate Afghan education efforts'. *Washington Post*, 23 March, p. A01.

Stigler, J. W., R. Gallimore and J. Hiebert. (2000). 'Using video surveys to compare classrooms and teaching across cultures: examples and lessons from the TIMSS video studies'. *Educational Psychologist*, 35(2), 87–100.

Stiglitz, J. E. (2002). *Globalization and Its Discontents*. New York: W. W. Norton.

Tacchi, J. & Slater, D. (2004). Research: ICT Innovations for Poverty Reduction. New Delhi: UNESCO.

Talbot, D. (2008). $100 Laptop Program's New President. Technology Review, May 2. Retrieved from: http://www.technologyreview.com/business/20711/. Last accessed on 12 September 2012.

Tausch, A. (2010). 'Passive globalization and the failure of the European Union's Lisbon Strategy, 2000–2010: some new cross-national evidence'. *Alternatives: Turkish Journal of International Relations*, 9(1).

Thapa, D. and S. Sijapati. (2004). *Kingdom under Siege: Nepal's Maoist Insurgency, 1996–2003*. London: Zed Books.

Therkilsden, O. (2000). Public sector reform in a poor, aid-dependent country, Tanzania. *Public Administration and Development*, 20, 61–71.

Tikly, L. (2001). 'Globalisation and education in the postcolonial world: towards a conceptual framework'. *Comparative Education*, 37(2), 151–71.

Tikly, L. and H. Dachi. (2009). 'The new regionalism in African education: limits and possibilities'. In L. Chisholm and G. Steiner-Khamsi (eds), *South-South Cooperation in Education and Development*. New York: Teachers College Press and Cape Town: HSRC Press.

Times Higher Education. (2004). World University Rankings 2004. Retrieved from www.timeshighereducation.co.uk/hybrid.asp?typeCode=153. Last accessed on 31 January 2012.

Times Higher Education. (2011). World University Rankings 2010–11. Retrieved from www.timeshighereducation.co.uk/world-university-rankings/2010–2011/top-200.html. Last accessed on 31 January 2012.

Tomlinson, J. (2000). 'Globalization and cultural identity'. In D. Held and A. McGrew (eds), *The Global Transformations Reader: An Introduction to the Globalization Debate*. Cambridge: Polity Press, pp. 269–77.

Tooley, J. (1997). Choice and diversity in education: A defence. *Oxford Review of Education,* 23(1), 103–16.

Trucano, M. (2005). *Knowledge Maps: ICT in Education*. Washington, DC: World Bank.

Trudell, B. (2009). 'Local-language literacy and sustainable development in Africa'. *International Journal of Educational Development*, 29, 73–9.

UNDP. (2004). *Nepal Human Development Report: Empowerment and Poverty Reduction*. Kathmandu: Author.

—. (2010). *The Real Wealth of Nations: Pathways to Human Development. Human Development Report 2010*. New York: Author.

UNESCO. (2000). *Education for All: The Year 2000 Assessment. Bangladesh Country Report*. Dhaka: Author.

—. (2003). *Gender and Education for All: The Leap to Equality*. Paris: Author.

—. (2005a). *Towards Knowledge Societies*. Paris: Author.

—. (2005b). 'United Nations decade of education for sustainable development (2005–2014): international implementation scheme'. Document ED/DESD/2005/PI/01. Paris: Author.

—. (2006). Education for All: Literacy for Life. Paris: Author.

—. (2008). *Education for all by 2015: Will we make it?* Oxford: Oxford University Press.

—. (2009). Overcoming Inequality: Why Governance Matters. Oxford: Oxford University Press.

—. (2010). *Reaching the Marginalized*. Oxford: Oxford University Press.

—. (2011). *The Hidden Crisis: Armed Conflict and Education*. Paris: Author.

UNESCO Institute for Statistics. (2005). Total expenditure on educational institutions and administration as a % of GDP. All sources. Primary. Retrieved from http://stats.uis.unesco.org/unesco/TableViewer/document.aspx?ReportId=136. Last accessed on 31 January 2012.

—. (2011a). Togo Country Profile. Retrieved from http://stats.uis.unesco.org/unesco/TableViewer/document.aspx?ReportId=121&BR_Country=7680

—. (2011b). Data Centre: Student Mobility Indicators. Retrieved from http://stats.uis.unesco.org

United Nations. (1948). *The Universal Declaration of Human Rights*. New York: Author.

—. (1961). 'United Nations Development decade: a programme for international economic co-operation'. United Nations General Assembly (sixteenth session). New York: Author.

—. (2000). United Nations Millennium Development Goals. Retrieved from www.un.org/millenniumgoals/education.shtml. Last accessed on 31 January 2012.

—. (2010). Investing in education will help advance global anti-poverty targets. Retrieved from www.un.org/apps/news/story.asp?NewsID=36081. Last accessed on 31 January 2012.

UNPD. (2009) The world urbanization prospects: the 2009 revision. Retrieved from http://esa.un.org/unpd/wup. Last accessed on 31 January 2012.

Upadhya, C. (2009). 'Imagining India: software and the ideology of liberalisation'. *South African Review of Sociology*, 40(1), 76–93.

USAID. (2004). Information and communication technology for development: USAID's worldwide progam. Washington, DC: USAID.

US Department of State. (2011). 2010 Human Rights Report: China. Retrieved from www.state.gov/g/drl/rls/hrrpt/2010/eap/154382.htm

US Joint Forces Command (2010). *The Joint Operating Environment*. Norfolk: Author.

Verger, A. (2009). 'The merchants of education: global politics and the uneven education liberalization process within the WTO'. *Comparative Education Review*, 53(3), 379–401.

Wagemaker, H. (2004). 'IEA: International studies, impact and transition'. Presented at the First IEA International Research Conference, 11–13 May 2004, Nicosia, Cyprus.

Wallerstein, I. (1974). *The Modern World System: Capitalist Agriculture and the Origins of the European World-Economy in the Sixteenth Century*. New York: Academic Press.

—. (1999). *The End of the World as We Know It*. Minneapolis: University of Minnesota Press.

Welch, A. (2002) 'Going global? Internationalizing Australian universities in a time of global crisis'. *Comparative Education Review*, 46(4), 433–71.

—. (2010). 'Vietnam, Malaysia and the global knowledge system'. In V. D. Rust, L. M. Portnoi and S. S. Bagley (eds), *Higher Education, Policy, and the Global Competition Phenomenon*. New York: Palgrave Macmillan, pp. 143–60.

West, A. and Ylönen, A. (2010). 'Market-oriented school reform in England and Finland: school choice, finance and governance'. *Educational Studies*, 36(1), 1–12.

Whelpton, J. (2005). *A History of Nepal.* Cambridge: Cambridge University Press.

Whitehouse. (2009). Educate to Innovate. Retrieved from www.whitehouse.gov/issues/education/educate-innovate. Last accessed on 31 January 2012.

—. (2011). Education. Retrieved from www.whitehouse.gov/issues/education. Last accessed on 20 December 2012.

World Bank (2001). 'Nepal: priorities and strategies for education reform'. Report No. 22065-NEP. Washington, DC: World Bank.

—. (2003a). *Lifelong Learning in the Global Knowledge Economy: Challenges for Developing Countries.* Washington, DC: World Bank.

—. (2003b). ICT for Development: Contributing to the millennium development goals. Washington, DC: World Bank.

—. (2009). KEI and KI Indexes. Retrieved from http://info.worldbank.org/etools/kam2/kam_page5.asp. Last accessed on 31 January 2012.

—. (2011). Poverty Reduction Strategies – What are PSRPs? Retrieved from http://go.worldbank.org/QP8TGIEM90. Last accessed on 31 January 2012.

—. (2012a). World Development Indicators: School enrollment, primary (%net). Retrieved from: http://data.worldbank.org/indicator/SE.PRM.NENR. Last accessed on 10 September 2012.

—. (2012b). World Development Indicators: School enrollment, primary, female (% net). Retrieved from http://data.worldbank.org/indicator/SE.PRM.NENR.FE. Last accessed on 10 September 2012.

World Bank Institute. (2008). *Measuring Knowledge in the World's Economies: Knowledge Assessment Methodology and Knowledge Economy Index.* Washington, DC: World Bank.

World Conference on Education for All. (1990). *World Declaration on Education for All and Framework to Meet Basic Learning Needs.* Paris: Author.

World Education Forum. (2000). *The Dakar Framework for Action.* Paris: Author.

World Summit on Information Society. (2003). Declaration of Principles. Document WSIS-03/GENEVA/DOC/4-E. United Nations World Summit on Information Society, 10–12 December, 2003, Geneva, Switzerland.

—. (2005). 'Tunis Commitment'. Document WSIS-05/TUNIS/DOC/7-E. United Nations World Summit on Information Society, 16–18 November 2005, Tunis, Algeria.

WTO. (2011a). The General Agreement on Trade in Services (GATS): objectives, coverage and disciplines. Retrieved from www.wto.org/english/tratop_e/serv_e/gatsqa_e.htm. Last accessed on 31 January 2012.

—. (2011b). Trade in Services Database. Retrieved from http://tsdb.wto.org/. Last accessed on 31 January 2012.

Index